T0199115

CHARLEY P. RINEY

A GUY NAMED
CHARLEY

MY REFUSAL TO BE AVERAGE

A GUY NAMED CHARLEY
MY REFUSAL TO BE AVERAGE

iUniverse books may be ordered through booksellers or by contacting:

iUniverse
1663 Liberty Drive
Bloomington, IN 47403
www.iuniverse.com
1-800-Authors (1-800-288-4677)

ISBN: 978-1-5320-6107-3 (sc)
ISBN: 978-1-5320-6108-0 (e)

Library of Congress Control Number: 2018913854

Print information available on the last page.

iUniverse rev. date: 11/19/2018

DEDICATION

This book is dedicated to my parents, Pat and Ruth Riney. Thanks for helping me become the man I am today. Also responsible for my character development and work ethic are my Uncle Tuck and all my coaches in high school, college, and even beyond. Thank you all.

ACKNOWLEDGEMENTS

First of all, my beautiful wife, Fran. Thanks for putting up with my hours in the office typing and swearing away.

For my former teaching colleague at Guilford High School, Mickey Swart. Thank you so much. Your insights, suggestions, editing, and proofreading are what made all this possible. Remember, you're the one who said, "You should write a book".

A special thank you to my good friends Pat Sullivan, Brigid Brausen, and Mike Papoccia for reading the early manuscripts and offering timely suggestions for improvement.

CHAPTER

ONE

My first heart attack was in June of 2006. I was teaching at Guilford High School in Rockford, Illinois, and it was graduation day. All the teachers were to be dressed in caps and gowns and were part of the processional entering and leaving the ceremony. Guilford is a large urban school of over 2,000 students, so the graduation was held in the Rockford Metro Center downtown to accommodate the large crowd. We faculty were bussed from the school to the site of graduation.

As I was putting on my gown, I began to suffer what I thought was intense heartburn. Heartburn had previously been a problem for me, so I wasn't overly concerned. I was taking prescription meds for the condition, so it was something of an ongoing problem. Several of us had gone out for lunch and had lost track of time and were compelled to wolf down our food in order to get to graduation on time, so I figured that was the problem.

The pain continued to worsen, and I went to the bathroom and sat on the toilet. I realized sweat was dripping from my nose like Lebron James in a playoff game. The pain was intense. It felt like a sumo wrestler was sitting on my chest. I started to think it may have been more than heartburn, but there were no other symptoms like radiating pain down my arm, pain in my neck, nausea, vomiting, shortness of breath, or dizziness. Just heartburn-like chest pain. Gradually it began to pass, and I joined my colleagues in time for the processional into the center. During the hour or so ceremony, I actually felt fine.

Afterwards we were bussed back to the high school, and I went to my classroom to gather a few items I was taking home. Guilford is obviously a large complex, and I had a lengthy walk to my exit and then to the parking lot. As I was making my way, the "heartburn" began again. Once again, there were no other symptoms other than chest pain. When I got to my car, I was again sweating profusely and had that invisible sumo guy on my chest again. I sat in my car for 20-25 minutes, and once again the pain subsided. I was scheduled to be in the office of my second job as a realtor, but I cancelled and went home. I took a couple of aspirin because I was beginning to wonder if a heart attack was my problem and then took a nap. When I awoke, the pain was again gone. My girlfriend, Fran (now my wife), had come to visit for the weekend and was more concerned than I. We ran to a nearby fast food joint for something to eat, but I didn't get anything because I wasn't hungry, and I was beginning to have discomfort--but no real pain.

About 3:30 or 4:00 in the morning, I woke up. I had been trying to sleep in a recliner because the pain had started again—not terrible, just annoying. I told Fran that something wasn't right, so we had better go to the hospital. She drove me to the ER at Swedish American Hospital, and I explained that I thought I was having a heart attack.

BAM! Within 3-4 minutes I was in a bed, hooked up to an EKG machine and surrounded by eleven people all very intent on making me feel better. I was soon in the catheter lab and having an angiogram. Like most people I had heard of an angiogram, but I wasn't exactly sure what the procedure was. The doctor, and nurses, were very informative. As I understood it, the doctor would numb my groin area and then a small tube (catheter) would be inserted into an artery. That catheter would be threaded through the system until it reached a coronary artery. Dye would then be injected through the catheter which makes it easy to see on X-ray images. As the dye moves through the blood vessels, the doctor can see its flow and identify any blockages. They discovered I had a 90% blockage of the left anterior descending artery (LAD), a blockage commonly known as the "widow-maker".

The next step was to insert a thin wire which was threaded through the catheter to the blockage. Over this wire, another catheter with a small expandable balloon on the end was passed to the blockage. The balloon was inflated, and it pushed the plaque (blockage) to the sides and stretched the artery open so blood can flow more easily. The next step was to insert a collapsed wire mesh tube (stent) on a special balloon over the wire to the blocked area. When this balloon was inflated, it opens the stent against the artery walls. The stent helps to keep the artery open. My docs inserted two stents, and then the catheters and balloon were removed.

They artery was open, and my heart could get the blood it needed. The tube used to place the stent was removed from the groin, direct pressure was applied, and one lies quietly flat for several hours and they checked for any signs of bleeding. Pretty amazing since I'm told the fatality rate for widow-maker clots is about 90%. Stents are incredibly common these days with hundreds of thousands placed every year. Still, above average.

As I had taught in the greater Rockford area for nearly thirty years, I encountered former students frequently in my various hospital visits. Nurses. CNAs, Technicians—met them all. One of my former students is the manager of the lab system at Swedish American Hospital. I've taught several students who became doctors, but none of them practice in the Rockford area.

The most "interesting" interaction occurred several years ago when I had had my first angiogram. In the process of sterilization prior to surgery, the entire groin area is shaved of all hair before being scrubbed and prepped. Imagine my surprise when a female former student entered and began to shave my groin. "Oh, hi, Mr. Riney. I haven't seen you in years. How have you been?" That's a difficult question to answer when a former student is shaving your scrotum! Certainly not an average occurrence.

If I remember correctly, I spent two days in the hospital following my "widow-maker" blockage and was released after the stents were placed. I felt great when I went home and soon began cardio rehab three days a week. It involved walking on a treadmill, riding a stationary bike, using a rowing machine, and very light weight work with resistance bands. It was closely monitored by taking blood sugar readings before and after workouts and pulse and blood pressure readings during the workouts. So pretty much my life was back to regular. I did think quite a bit about how and why I was able to "beat the odds" against surviving the widow-maker and couldn't help but wonder, "Why me?"

Maybe I have surmounted all my challenges and enjoyed all my blessings because I myself am above-average. I have expected and received the best—in all aspects of my life. It is said that we do not know how we will handle adversity until we are directly faced with it, but I have always felt that I would somehow triumph over difficulties. Maybe that attitude itself is above-average; there is no room for doubt in a positive-thinking life.

Most 60-year-olds have known several people in their lives who have passed away. A couple probably died from heart attacks. I know that was true in my case. I truly spent substantial time wondering why some die and some live. I started to become aware of my own mortality and it was a bit disconcerting. I was 60 years old, and I'd had a heart attack; what else might happen?

For several year back in the late '70s, I had several symptoms similar to rheumatoid arthritis. However, the terrible joint pain I experienced would vary nearly daily: Monday the left wrist, Tuesday the right elbow, Wednesday the right fingers and hand, Thursday the left hand, and so on. After a battery of tests, the doctors were certain I did not have arthritis. They were fairly certain I had lupus, but there weren't enough "markers" present to definitively make the diagnosis.

Lupus is a chronic inflammatory disease that occurs when the body's immune system attacks its own tissues and organs. Why one's body attacks itself isn't known, and lupus is incurable, but in most cases, it's controllable. The inflammation caused by lupus can affect many different body systems: joints, skin, blood cells, brain, heart, and lungs. Lupus is difficult to diagnose because the signs and symptoms can be so similar to other ailments. The episodes when signs and symptoms get worse for a while are called flares. Because it attacks some of the major organs in the body, in a worst-case scenario, lupus can be fatal. Lupus is eight times more common in women than men and nine times more likely to affect blacks than whites. (I guess I'm just a big, black woman inside.) Ironically, my wife is black, and both she and her sister suffer from lupus.

In the fall of 1984, I had experienced a flare of my lupus-like symptoms. I spent a month in the local hospital, and the doctors determined that I was definitely suffering from lupus. In addition to the severe joint pain, my kidneys were being affected. A common remedy for kidney issues is the corticosteroid prednisone. I was given 100 mg daily for a couple of weeks. One of the side effects is weight gain. I gained sixty pounds in less than a week; I was swollen everywhere. I was then transported to the Mayo Clinic in Rochester, Minnesota, where I spent another week. While I was there, they performed a renal (kidney) biopsy, and my kidneys were found to be nearly shut down. The prednisone gradually got my kidneys functioning again, and I returned home. If, for example, normal kidney function is in the range of 5-7, mine has been about 4.6 for years. Slightly below the norm. I haven't needed dialysis, but I do see a kidney specialist several times a year, and my kidney's efficiency is now gradually deteriorating. The bottom line is my kidneys haven't been fully functioning in over thirty years. I didn't realize at the time the far-reaching effects lupus would have on my health.

CHAPTER

TWO

As a young man, I had been very active, especially in sports. I was always the tallest in my class, and by my senior year in high school, I stood 6'6". I was one of the fortunate ones to receive a full scholarship to attend college because of my basketball skills. I was the first of my family to ever attend (and graduate) from college. Both of my parents were high school dropouts. Dad had been an artillery sergeant in the Army during WWII. I remember him proudly recalling how "his guys" were able to "get five in the air." That means they were able to fire five shots so quickly the first round hadn't yet impacted. However, he developed such terrible ulcers that he was given a medical discharge and a pension before his unit was sent overseas. He came home and got a decent job in a local factory. Mom stayed at home which was like the moms of all my friends. I don't remember a single mother of anyone in school whose mother had a job. This was back in the late '40s and '50s, the golden era of middle-class America.

At the end of my first season of college basketball, the track coach convinced me to go out for track and try the high jump. The old cliché that "white men can't jump" did not apply to me. I could really sky. By my senior year in track, I held some meet records, was conference champion, and was twice invited to the prestigious Central Collegiate Championships. Junior year the CCC was at Notre Dame, and senior year it was at Marquette. I also qualified for the NCAA finals my senior year by placing fourth at the NCAA Midwest Regional track meet. That was for colleges in Iowa, Illinois, Missouri, Colorado, Nebraska, Wisconsin, Minnesota, and Indiana. State College of Iowa (SCI), now University of Northern Iowa (UNI), had an indoor and outdoor meet for all the colleges in Iowa except for Iowa, Iowa State, and Drake. My senior year I won the high jump at both the indoor and outdoor meets, making me the unofficial college high jump champion of Iowa colleges. I ended up with 7 varsity letters in basketball and track. Not bad for a skinny kid from a small Catholic high school in Keokuk, Iowa. Certainly, an above average career.

I share these achievements to illustrate how I have been successful in so many ways. I expected to be successful in everything I attempted. The discipline and work ethic that athletic success instilled in me most definitely carried over into other aspects of my life.

One of my college basketball teammates was diagnosed with cancer many years ago. He was given a few months to live. As he explained to us one weekend when several of us got together, "I'm not average. I'm taller than average [he was 6'8"], my grades say I'm smarter than average, I was a straight A student in high school, I got A's in engineering in college, I went to college free because of my basketball skills, which isn't average. My success in the business world is evidence I'm above average. Well, the average guy might die in a few months, but I'm not average. I'm going to live for years." And he did live for another thirty years or so. His attitude impressed me and several of my friends and teammates. Without realizing it, I have subconsciously adopted his great view of life. I'm not average dammit. The widow-maker might get 90% of those average guys, but it damn sure isn't going to get me.

CHAPTER
THREE

I guess one's DNA and family tree play some part in making us the way we are. According to the Ancestry.com DNA test, I'm 65% Irish, 12% Western European, 12% Scandanavian, 5% English, and 2-3% a couple of others. Growing up, I'd always been told we were related to Daniel Boone, but we really had no proof. A few years ago, one of our cousins who is deep onto genealogy, did scads of research on the Rineys. He discovered my great-great- grandmother's obituary from the Quincy, Illinois *Herald Whig:*

> Friday, December 18, 1908, Police Officer Patrick Riney [my grandfather, a police officer in Quincy, IL] returned home yesterday afternoon from St. Patrick, Missouri, where he went to attend the funeral of his grandmother, Mrs. Rose Simpson Riney. A niece of the famous Daniel Boone, whose name has come down through history as a pioneer frontiersman in Kentucky in the early days of the nation. She died at peace last Friday at the extreme age of 99, 50 years to the day after the death of her husband, Richard Riney, a pioneer settler of Missouri. Mrs. Riney

was born in Kentucky on July 19, 1810, only a few years after her uncle had wrested that part of the country away from the Indians and afterwards made part of the United States. Her mother was a sister of Daniel Boone.

While a young girl her family moved from Kentucky to Sangamon County, Illinois. She married Richard Riney on her twentieth birthday and that same year they took up a government claim and moved to Clark County, Missouri, and helped to establish the small community of St. Patrick, Missouri, where Mrs. Riney lived for 76 years. For the past 26 years she had lived on the same farm with Mrs. Rebecca Riney, Officer Patrick Riney's mother. She had been a member of St. Patrick parish for 75 years and had labored with her own hands in assisting to build the first house of worship in St. Patrick.

Mrs. Riney was well known for her wide charities and deep piety and was loved because of her amiable and gentle disposition. She was known by nearly everyone for miles around St. Patrick, and when the funeral was held, nearly the entire population in that section turned out to attend the obsequies, and the services were attended by far with the largest number of people that had ever been in attendance at any similar ceremony in St. Patrick here to fore.

> Man! Ya gotta love the way they wrote obituaries over a hundred years ago. I never met her but heard many tales of her as I was growing up. She was not an average person by any stretch of the imagination.

The other "family legend" was that a several times great-uncle had taught Abraham Lincoln. That information was validated in Carl Sandburg's book, *The Prairie Years*. A man named Zachariah Riney and a man named Caleb Hazel taught in the one-room schoolhouse Abraham Lincoln attended.

Again, according to my cousin, the Riney family moved from Maryland to Kentucky when Zachariah was about thirty years of age. When he taught the school where Abraham Lincoln attended he was about fifty years of age. Riney sold his land and bought about 1,000 acres and farmed until he died at the age of 96. His son, Sylvester Riney, then donated land for the Illinois Central Railroad right of way in 1874. The community which grew next to the railroad was named Rineyville as a sign of respect. Rineyville, Kentucky still exists and is a community of 6,000 people.

CHAPTER

FOUR

I know very little about my mother's side of the family – the Cockrells. My mother's brother had done some research, but the knowledge was not terribly revealing. Apparently, there were two Cockrell brothers who were lawyers in Missouri when the Civil War broke out. They both joined the Confederate army. One was a colonel and was severely wounded early in the war. The other was a brigadier general who was wounded six times while serving for four years.

According to my uncle, the brigadier general was a big man for the time—over six feet. During one battle as his troops were losing, he rode up and down behind the line with his saber in one hand and a magnolia blossom in the other encouraging his men. Allegedly his men responded and jumped up from their cover and attacked the enemy winning the engagement.

After the war, both men returned to practicing law. One in Missouri, and one in Texas. The colonel (Texas) was elected to the U.S. Congress and served for seven years. His son became a judge and eventually founded the Southern Methodist University School of Law.

General Cockrell was elected to the United States Senate from Missouri and served there for thirty years. One of his sons graduated from Harvard University and also became a judge. He wrote numerous books on world peace and justice and was once nominated for the Noble Peace Prize. He did not win. Still, far above average.

About the only other thing I know from my mother's side is my maternal grandfather, Charley Cockrell, after whom I was named, drove a gas delivery truck, and my grandmother, Nellie, was a stay-at-home mom. I've learned that Grandpa Charley received a draft notice during WWII... when he was 59! This illustrates how it was "everyone aboard" during the War. He did not go into service. My mother was one of four children. Her brother, my Uncle Homer, always took a perverse glee in recounting that they had a relative who had been hanged in Kansas for stealing a horse. (Can't beat some diversity in your DNA.)

When talking about ancestors over whom one has absolutely no control, one has to take the bad with the good. Apparently four Riney brothers--James, John, Thomas, and Jonathan, eventually a Revolutionary War soldier--came to America to find a better life in the late 1700s. Many of the Rineys migrated to Kentucky, and Thomas became the progenitor of the branch who remained there and sired such notables as Zachariah Riney, previously explained as the first schoolteacher of Abraham Lincoln.

Not all the Rineys back then were as high caliber as Zachariah. Allegedly, an Andy Jack Riney, who farmed in the St. Patrick, Missouri, area died at the age of 38 while inebriated. The story goes that he was out drinking with friends, and they stopped at a store. Andy remained outside and when his friends returned, they discovered him dead. While examining the body his friends discovered a bottle of whiskey in his pocket. They took it out and drank it before further attending to his body. Doubtful that was average behavior.

I share this Riney background because I guess part of what makes me, me, is the gene pool from which I've descended. I truly believe that we really have no right to brag about our ancestors because we certainly have nothing to do with their achievements or their foibles. However, part of me can't help but think that ol' Zachariah Riney may somehow be a reason I went into education and taught high-school English for forty-seven years. It's also interesting to know that a couple of my ancestors died from heart attacks. Going back to my college teammate's philosophy, they may have been a little too average.

I had never put my thoughts into words until my friend explained to me his "philosophy of average." I'm not average, so things that affect average people in a sense don't apply to me. I don't mean to sound arrogant, or entitled, or better than others. I guess I have higher standards for my behavior, my performance, and in my reactions to things that happen to me. I realized it was what I had sort of subconsciously felt for years. I began to form my own way of looking at my life and adapted a much more positive attitude because I know I'm not average in the sense that I had had such wonderful and life-changing opportunities up to the point of my first heart attack that most people never experience. My philosophy was something like, "Don't worry. I got this. No matter what it is, I can handle it—perhaps others can't, but I can.

CHAPTER

FIVE

I started playing organized basketball in 5th grade. In both 5th and 6th grade, I was pathetic: skinny, no coordination. I was terrible. But, I was tall. I played and loved it. By the 7th and 8th grades, I had improved to where I was just bad. But I still had the advantage of height: 5'10" in the 8th grade. In one 8th-grade game I scored six points, which was about as many as I scored in all my previous games combined. Like I said, I was bad.

During the summer between 8th and 9th grades, something happened which made me realize I could jump. While playing in a pick-up game at our local high school gym, my opponent faked a shot, and I jumped to block it. Much to my surprise, I hit my hand on the rim. It was a "light bulb" moment. I was ecstatic. Wow, I could jump! Next goal became dunking the ball. (Which I was able to do as a sophomore.) Before this epiphany, I had never tried to see how high I could jump, but from then on, I started trying to improve my jumping ability.

When basketball season began my 9th grade year, I had grown to 6'2" and weighed a rail-thin, whopping 145 pounds.. From the side, if I stuck out my tongue I looked like a zipper. But by the end of the season I was starting on the sophomore team and even dressed for several varsity games, in which I actually scored a couple of varsity points.

When I was about a year old, I had fallen off my parents' bed and broken my left collarbone. In July between 9th and 10th grade, I broke my left collarbone again playing baseball with a bunch of my friends. In September of that year I broke it again playing touch football. The doctor decided to operate and insert a steel pin to strengthen it. I missed half of the basketball season before I was cleared to play. I was now 6'4" and a halfway decent player. My shoulder area was heavily taped in order to protect my collarbone. One night I forgot to apply the gauze before it was taped. After the game, as I started to pull off the tape, it hurt like hell. My buddy, Tim Hickey, boldly said, "Don't be a sissy. Just rip it off." I did, tearing the scar off and leaving me in tears from pain I can't describe. I ended up in the ER and then had a skin graft where the scar tissue used to be. Despite that excruciating incident, probably the highlight of the season was the fact that I was now able to dunk.

My junior year I was 6'5", 175, and a varsity starter. I remember vividly the first game of the season. The smell of popcorn in the gym, the cheerleaders trying to whip the home team's fans into a frenzy. It was great. I scored 20 points and had 12 rebounds, but we lost. That was a pattern that would continue. On a couple of occasions, I literally scored half of our team's points, but we lost. We were not a good team overall and ended with an 8-13 record. Personally, the season was successful. I was named first team All-Conference and ended up averaging a double-double, 13 points, and 11 rebounds.

Senior year was amazing. Most of our good players were returning, and hopes were high. We started off 8-2. The season was exciting, and I still have great memories of games, practices, and the amazing camaraderie that sports, particularly in a small town in the Midwest, develops. We were 2nd in the conference, won the district tournament, and finished with a 15-5 record. My statistics were again a double-double and All-Conference, but my friend and teammate Dick Logsdon actually led our team in scoring and was also All-Conference.

CHAPTER
SIX

In the beginning of the season, I began to receive letters from colleges, which ignited the recruiting process. The first school to contact me was St. Louis University. Over the course of the season, I also heard from Iowa State University, the University of Iowa, the University of Denver, Loras College, St. Ambrose College, Buena Vista College, Bradley University, and Marquette University. In those days, the NCAA did not have a Division I, II, and III set-up as they do today. At that time, there was the University Division and the College Division. If College Division schools had the financial wherewithal and desire, they could offer full scholarships just like the big schools in the University Division. University and college schools were able to offer partial scholarships as well. Today, Division I schools in men's basketball and football can only offer full rides, no partials. Division II schools can offer full or partial scholarships, but not as many as Division I schools. Division III schools are not permitted to offer athletic scholarships.

As the first one in my family to attend college, my dilemma was whether to accept a partial scholarship from a big school or take the full ride from a small school like Loras College. I opted for the full ride from

Loras in Dubuque, Iowa, since we simply didn't have the finances to pay for even part of a college education. Without basketball, I'd never have been able to go to college.

Fifty years later with decades of experiences in high school coaching behind me and having been blessed to have had several athletes who were recruited at the scholarship level, including both of my sons, I remain amazed that Richard Logsdon, my high-school teammate and friend, also received a scholarship to St. Ambrose College in Davenport, Iowa. We actually played against each other twice a year. Loras and St. Ambrose were arch rivals. We had thirty-three students in our high-school graduating class, 150 students in the entire school, and we had two scholarship athletes. I can't imagine the odds against that. Our little school was in Keokuk, Iowa, not Chicago, or Detroit, or some other basketball hotbed.

When I look back, I realize we played some great competition. Some of our better opponents included 6'4" Mike Putnam of Walsh High School in Ottumwa, Iowa, who was the all-time leading scorer and rebounder in Iowa high-school history when to he graduated. He's in the Iowa Basketball Hall of Fame. He went to the Air Force Academy, transferred to St. Louis University, and ended up at Parsons College. Gary Olson 6'6" of Olds High School is also in the Iowa Hall of Fame. He started for a couple of years at the University of Iowa. Don Walljasper 6'4" of St. Mary's High School in West Point, Iowa was a scholarship player at St. Ambrose. Dave Coffman 6'4" from Dallas City, Illinois, was a player at Kenosha College in Wisconsin. In addition, Greg Douglas, 6'9", was a Parade All American at Keokuk High School, and we played with and against him many, many times in pick-up games. Greg went to the University of Kansas.

Despite our statistics and achievements, neither Dick Logsdon nor I were gifted natural athletes. We worked our butts off during the season, the off-season, and especially the summer. I can't begin to estimate how many hundreds—perhaps thousands—of hours we spent playing basketball. The place to be was Huiskamp's outdoor court, which was on the other side of town. As freshmen and sophomores (before driver's licenses), we would walk the two miles or so each way and play for hours. We would actually take shovels with us (later when cars were involved) and clean the snow off the court so we could play. When a game was finished, everyone would jam into the cars to get warm for the next game. It was pretty well known that "Logger" and Riney were ready, willing, and able to play anywhere, anytime.

In the summer before I left for college, my mother was slowly dying of ovarian cancer. I don't remember if it was Coach Cronin or Father Stratman, the parish priest, but one of them gave me a key to the gym. I lived only three blocks away. To work off stress, anxiety, and concern for my mother, I used to go to the gym late at night and shoot, all alone, for hours. It was really a double blessing because I also was able to work on my game. She died on August 3, 1963, a few weeks before I left for Loras College.

CHAPTER

SEVEN

Another crucial part of my background that has certainly helped make me who I am today is my uncle's farm. From before I can remember until I was in high school, my brother Bill, my sister Becky, and I spent a week or several weeks each summer on my uncle's farm in Missouri. My dad's sister, Aunt Ethel, and her husband, Tuck, lived about fifteen miles from Hannibal, Missouri. His real name was Francis, but Aunt Ethel was the only one I ever heard call him Francis. He was from Kentucky, hence the name Tuck.

Most of my friends and family know I hate fowl. I refuse to eat it: all kinds--chicken, duck, goose, Cornish hen, quail, pheasant. If it has feathers, I won't eat it. I'm also "afraid" of birds. A bird in the house for example, flitting about and dive-bombing terrifies me. Crazy, right? Well, here's the behind-the-scenes full story.

When I was about four or five years old, Uncle Tuck created "lassoes" of binder twine--loose, floppy string—for Bill and me. We were then allowed to attempt to rope a chicken. There were dozens of white Leghorn chickens and a couple of roosters. Against about a billion to one odds, I lassoed one of the big ol' roosters, which was about as tall as I. Instead of trying to get away as the twine tightened around its neck, this damn rooster turned and attacked me. As I said, it was my size and began beating me with its wings, pecking at me, and trying to get me with his spurs. I remember being knocked to the ground and rolling over to protect myself and get away from this monster. This rooster kicked my ass! It's funny to people now, but it obviously scarred me psychologically for life.

On a more positive note, farm life for me as a city kid was great. There were hogs, cattle, sheep, lots of corn, soybeans, and other crops. Best of all, they had riding horses. Bill and I spent hours and hours riding all over the nearly one thousand acres, many acres of which were timber. I remember vividly there were two black quarter horses, Joe and Smokey, we weren't allowed to ride. Uncle Tuck limited us to a chesnut gelding named Dick. We weren't allowed to use a saddle but had to learn bare back. Whenever we fell off, which was common, ol' Dick would instantly stop. My uncle wanted us to learn bare back, so we could feel the rhythm and gait of the horse. The next summer, when we were allowed to saddle up, it was like riding a rocking horse. My younger sister, Becky, was compelled to help Aunt Ethel virtually all day, every day. The farm had four ponds, each with a different mixture of bass, bluegills, catfish, perch, and crappie. It was heaven. However, the lifestyle of rural Missouri in the late 1940s and early 1950s was quite rustic. I remember when they had no electricity and used kerosene lanterns for illumination. They never had running water, and as late as 1962, they still had a pump on the well and an outhouse. I'm probably one of the few people alive today who have churned butter by hand from milk/cream that I had obtained earlier in the day by milking a cow. When we weren't running around, fishing, riding, or later on, working in the fields, we spent countless hours on the front porch with Aunt Ethel snapping beans or shelling peas—a very boring pastime. As mentioned, Becky, wasn't as lucky as Bill and me. She spent most of her days helping Aunt Ethel with household chores and other "woman's work". Their garden was humongous, about five acres, and Aunt Ethel canned hundreds of jars of veggies to be eaten every year.

I'd bet if you looked up "work ethic" in the dictionary, you'd find a picture of my Uncle Tuck. What a great guy. Up at 5:00 every morning, milking cows and feeding livestock seven days a week. Monday through

Saturday he worked a 12-hour day. He was a lean, mean, working machine. His leathery, vise-grip hands were amazing. Uncle Tuck was about 6'0" and lean and sinewy. He was in his 60s at the time but could out work a 20-year-old under the table. His standards were high when we were doing chores. "Good enough" was never acceptable when a task should be "done right." That's become part of my work philosophy ever since. Uncle Tuck was also full of "down home" words and expressions. One of his favorites, which cracked Bill and me up every time was, "That's slicker than hog snot on a wet board." I couldn't make this stuff up.

When I was about four years old, I remember sitting on his lap and talking about his eye, and glasses. As a young man, Tuck had had a piece of wood from a chunk he was chopping fly into his eye. It literally put his eye out. He never wore an eye patch, but had a hole there, where the eyeball used to be. We never thought it was gross or scary. It was just Uncle Tuck. For some reason, as I was sitting on his lap, I grabbed his glasses and threw them to the floor. Wham, bam! He damn sure didn't ask for permission from my parents but turned me over and proceeded to beat my little butt. Years later it was a family story, about "the time Uncle Tuck beat you for grabbing his glasses."

One cool thing was when Bill and I were about nine or ten, we were put to work…driving a tractor. We drove slowly down the windrow of hay bales in the field while the grown men tossed the bales onto the wagon for the "stacker" to arrange. It was nearly beyond our comprehension: getting to drive a tractor at nine or ten. Now that's obviously common for farm kids, but we were city kids. Our friends back in Keokuk were eating their hearts out with jealousy. As we grew older each year, our responsibilities increased to disking, dragging a harrow, and even plowing. I'm so thankful I got to be a part-time farmer in my youth under the watchful eye and high standards of Uncle Tuck. He formed a significant part of my way of looking at life. He was certainly far above-average, even though I didn't fully realize it at the time.

CHAPTER

EIGHT

In September of 1963, I arrived at Loras College in Dubuque, Iowa. At that time Loras was a small Catholic liberal arts college of 1,400 men only. Our sister institution of all women was Clarke College, located several blocks away. Both schools are now co-ed. Loras was very much "old school" even for the times. By today's standards, it was downright monastic. For example, we were required to wear a suit coat to dinner each evening. We didn't have to eat breakfast, but we were required to go through the line and check in between 6 and 8:00 am on Monday through Friday. No sleeping in and wasting time. "Idleness is the devil's workshop" we were reminded. Only two of the 1,400 students were non-Catholics. The rest of us were required to attend Mass three times each week, plus Sunday. We had assigned seats in the chapel, and one of the priests took roll. Amazingly, as college freshmen we had curfews. There was a bed check each night at 10:00 pm. If a student wasn't in his room, he was in big trouble. Being in the bathroom was NOT an acceptable excuse. Father Kutsch, Dean of Students, lived in our dorm and performed the bed check himself. However, on Fridays we had a midnight curfew and had to sign-in before midnight in the dorm's reception area. We were permitted to stay out until midnight one other night. Most of us wanted it to be Saturday, provided we got up between 7-8:00 am that Saturday morning and went to the Dean's office to request permission. We also had maid service to sweep out our rooms, clean up the sinks, and make the beds, but not on Thursdays. On Thursdays when Father Kutsch took bed check, unmade beds led to more big trouble.

So, what was the "big trouble?" What was the punishment levied on college freshmen for these grievous offenses? It was the dreaded "5:50." That meant students had to get up, be fully dressed (even socks), and go to the dorm registration area and sign one's name and room number at 5:50 AM. Then students were free to go back to bed or whatever. Some transgressions might merit a sentence of three, four, or five 5:50s in a row. For more serious offenses, or for "too many" 5:50s, students had to go sign in at one of the other dorms on the other side of campus. The Loras campus is built on a very steep hill, so this type of 5:50 meant lots of stairs. It was horrible. All the students were fatigued for the first couple of weeks every year. And then there was something called a campus. That meant from 6:00 AM until 6:00 PM one had to sign in every half hour – at Keane Hall (top of the hill) on the hour, and at Beckman Hall (bottom of the hill) on the half hour. After an hour or two, one's legs were so tired and cramping from all the stairs it took nearly the entire half hour to get from one dorm to the other. It was a real killer. This was especially true in the winter, when the wind was howling, and the snow was swirling. If one is familiar with Dubuque, the "hawk" (wind) seems to always be out. I personally never was given a campus, but my roommate, Joe Heiple, spent nearly every other Saturday trudging up and down the hilly campus to sign-in at Keane and Beckman Halls.

I was assigned to live in Keane Hall, 2nd floor, and had two roommates. One was Joe Hajek from Flint, Michigan. He was on a half-basketball, half-track-scholarship, and he was a stud. He was the rare athlete who was both quick and fast. He's in the 1,000 point club in basketball and 50 years later still holds the Loras school record in the quarter-mile. His senior year he finished second in the NCAA National Track & Field Championships. Joe was inducted into the Loras Athletic Hall of Fame in 1993.

My other roommate was Joe Heiple from Waterloo, Iowa, and he was a fun guy. Practical jokes and goofing off in the dorm were his apparent majors. He left Loras after a year but later went to get not only a bachelor's but also his master's degree and had a long and successful career as a teacher. In fact, I believe he was once named Iowa's Teacher of the Year. Amazingly, he and I ran into each other six years later in Vietnam and served together for about 10 months. Joe passed away a couple of years ago.

CHAPTER
NINE

I have always been a competitive person. I don't like to lose. I also never allowed my children to beat me in anything just to "be nice." When, and if, they beat me in chess, driveway basketball, or anything, they knew they had earned it. One of my grandsons, Rowan, recently told me thanks for not letting him win after I had taught him to play chess when he was in kindergarten. When he finally beat me years later, it was like Christmas for him. His desire to beat Grandpa helped drive him to practice, read about chess, join a chess club, and become an excellent player. How good? Well, now the shoe is on the other foot. He's a superb player. Recently he tied for first place in a huge tournament which was mostly adults, in St. Louis where he lives. His share of the first-place prize was $750. He's now 15 and in high school. We played again this past Christmas, and he beat me in a matter of minutes. He then offered to play me while blindfolded. I most definitely turned down the offer and went off to lick my destroyed ego.

So, when basketball practice began formally in October 1963, my competitive juices were flowing. Our freshman class was made up of some excellent players. We had size and speed, inside power and outside shooting. We had players from all over the Midwest: Michigan, Minnesota,

Illinois, and Iowa. Most were like me and had taken the full scholarship from Loras rather than a partial scholarship from a major university. After weeks of practice, the season began with the annual Varsity vs. Freshman game. One of the first things I had realized was different from high school was when our trainer, Doc Kammer, took one look at me and said, "Damn, Riney. You need to drink a couple of beers every night to gain some weight." Like most high schools, we had had rules that if a player was caught drinking, there was a long suspension as punishment. Now, in college, they were telling me to drink a couple of beers every night. Didn't seem average.

CHAPTER
TEN

After weeks of practice and anticipation, the day of the Freshmen vs Varsity game finally arrived. It was held in the old Loras Fieldhouse. The place was rocking. The student body was raucous, loud, and in a frenzy before the game even started. For many of them, their pre-game routine was in a local pub. The varsity, with their experience, was favored, but everyone knew we had a number of talented players, so an upset wasn't out of the question. After fifty years I can still remember the smell of popcorn, the sound of the crowd roaring, the band playing during warm-ups. It still gives me tingles.

I was a starter for the freshmen, and my match-up on defense was big Fred Kunnert, a senior who was listed at 6'4" and 250 lbs. He was a big dude, but incredibly agile and quick for a man his size. He was a returning varsity starter and I was a 6'6", 190-pound freshman. On about the third trip down the floor the varsity passed the ball into Fred on the low post. I knew his favorite shot was a sweet hook shot. He faked one way and stepped into the hook. Bam! I jumped and literally blocked the ball into the balcony in the old Loras Fieldhouse. The crowd went bananas. I was feeling pretty good about myself.

On their next possession, Fred again posted low, got the ball and stepped into his hook shot. Up I went, and he pulled down the ball and went up for a jump shot, leading with his giant, meaty elbow. It collided with my face, the foul was on me, and I went to the trainer's room for two stitches to close the bloody cut above my right eye. OK, lesson learned, Freshman. This wasn't going to be so easy after all. I was able to return and play after being attended to, which was different from high-school ball. In high school, I would most likely have been held out for the duration of the game.

We played well and nearly won the game, losing by five points if memory serves me right. Years later, our coach, Dick Wright, confessed to me he had taken the press off, with which the varsity had struggled. Joe Hajec, Rex Hester, and Jeff Gadient—our guards, were all quick, and the varsity was struggling. However, because he didn't want us to beat the varsity and be compelled to go through the hell on earth the varsity coach, Bob Zahren, would have inflicted on us all, we stopped pressing late in the game.

Coach Wright had been a great player at Loras. He's in the Loras Athletic Hall of Fame and the 1,000 point club. During my junior year in high school, he coached at our arch-rival, Aquinas High School in Fort Madison, Iowa. By my senior year he was freshman coach at Loras and recruited me heavily. Years later, I became great friends with him, and we became very close. Coach passed away all too soon in 2009 after a long battle with leukemia. He was an amazing man who was still playing full-court basketball into his 70s.

Our head varsity coach was Bob Zahren. Coach Zahren's true expertise had been in football, and he was tough as nails. He had been a great football player for Chicago Mt. Carmel High School. He was a Marine during WWII and a College Division All-American football guard as a player at Loras. When the college dropped football in the 1950s, Coach Zahren moved over as basketball coach. He was one tough son-of-a gun. We actually almost felt sorry for the Germans he had faced in WWII. To be honest, we were all scared to death of him.

His practices were beyond description. Defense was his favorite aspect, and he wanted us to play nearly as if it were indoor football. The players called him "Bubzy"--never to his face. Bob Z = Bub zy or Bubz. His two-a-day practices in the early part of the season and during Christmas break were so physically demanding they defy explanation. Once when we returned from a road trip loss at 2 or 3:00 in the morning, he ordered us into the gym and to practice for a couple of hours. He was obviously not happy with how we had played. When I was in basic training in the army at Fort Polk in Louisiana, I frequently thought back to the times I'd been through practice with Coach Z. Honestly, military basic training was physically and emotionally less demanding than his basketball practices had been. Once again, no "average" person would have been able to make it through his difficult regimen. In my mind, I believed what the army was throwing at me wasn't as tough as what I'd been through under Coach Zahren. Thanks so much, Coach, for making me more competitive and giving me that hard-nosed attitude which refuses to quit whether it be a game, a job, the military, or battling health issues. We were all terrified of the man as student-athletes, but years later I got to know him adult-to-adult. He was a hell of a guy. I hadn't seen him for several years, but a few years ago my wife, Fran, and I were back at Loras for Homecoming. We decided to drop by his house, and we had a couple of hours of great "catch up" conversation about what had been going on in our lives. He passed away a few months later.

One of my proudest athletics moments came my sophomore year, and it involved Coach Zahren. We were playing Iowa Wesleyan at home. Wesleyan's best players were Frank Dexter-- who went on to become a very successful high school basketball coach, notably at Moline High School in Illinois—and Davey Lopes, their point guard. Yes, *that* Davey Lopes: the one who was drafted by the Los Angeles Dodgers, played second base for them, and played in the 1974, 1977, and 1978 World Series, and won the World Series championship with the Dodgers in 1981. Davey was a four-time All-Star and stole forty bases at the age of forty. He coached and managed until 2017. He's now retired.

I had started that particular game but was on the bench as the game wore down. Suddenly Coach Zahren came down to me, pulled me up, and said, "Charley, be an All-American and go in there and win us this game." Now if that didn't get my adrenalin pumped like two Mountain Dews and a 5-Hour Energy drink, I don't know what would.

CHAPTER
ELEVEN

In our first regular game after the varsity exhibition, we played another freshmen team in the dedication of their new gym. One of their top players was a 6'4" kid from Chicago. I've mentioned before that I could really jump, but he could jump with a capital "J". The first time I got the ball and went up for a jump shot, he caught the ball in the crook of his elbow. To make matters worse, he had a jingle bell about the size of a golf ball on each shoe--not legal today, but it was back then. As a result, I could hear those damn bells all night, always looking to see where he was. It was an absolutely phenomenal psychological weapon. Wish I'd thought of it. Our freshman team was pretty successful, and we finished the season with a record of 13-5.

Sophomore year, we had only two seniors, and all the rest of us were sophomores and green as hell. Six-foot, six-inch point guard Laddie Sula had played varsity as a freshman, but the rest of us had played on the freshman team. I started as a sophomore and had a decent year with a couple of highlights like the Wesleyan game, but as a team we were not very successful. We won a total of seven games.

At the start of my junior year, expectations were high because we had virtually everyone returning and some excellent recruits. I started and had an acceptable season with a few highlights. We improved to winning eight games that season. Perhaps the biggest news was that Coach Zahren resigned in the middle of the season. Assistant coach Jerry Potts took over and was named head coach for the following season.

For senior year, the 1966-67 season, anticipation of a great season was high. We had a new coach, Coach Potts, we returned the entire starting team, we had a couple of great freshman prospects, and we were to be playing in the new Midlands Conference, which was made up of some of the best small college basketball programs in the Midwest: Quincy University, Lewis University, St. Ambrose University, St. Norbert's, and a couple more. Personally, I had grown an inch since junior year and was now 6'7" and 215 pounds. However, one of those great freshmen prospects, Tommy Jackson, 6'6" from Chicago's Dunbar High School, took my starting position. Tommy went on to have a phenomenal career, and when he graduated, he was Loras's all-time leading rebounder--and still is 48 years later. At that time, he was 3rd all-time scorer with 1,619 points. His senior year he was an All-American, so I tell people I got beat out by an All-American. Dr. Thomas Jackson is in the Loras Hall of Fame.

Senior year was great. Awesome memories. We finished 18-10 and won the conference championship. We also finished second in a Christmas tournament at UW-LaCrosse, losing to Lincoln University of Missouri. They were really good. In fact, they placed second in the NCAA College Division national tournament later that year and had three players drafted into the pros. Their best player was Arvesta Kelly, who played for five years in the ABA. We also qualified for the national tournament of the NAIA (National Association of Intercollegiate Athletics). I have so many fond memories of the games, the practices, and mostly the guys. Sula, Gadink, Cons, Tommy D., Baron, Duke, Bullet, Chip, Ginny, Skin, Hajey, Rex, Tommy J., and Brett. Great nicknames for great guys. I'm prejudiced but I think our fourteen players and four-year student manager were one of the best examples of true "student athletes" one will ever find. Since college graduation, team members have gone on to earn five PhDs, and nearly everyone else has a master's degree. One of my teammates, Dr. Chip Barder, recently retired as the Head of the United Nations International

School of Hanoi. Prior to that he was Head of International schools in the Congo, Malaysia, Indonesia, Syria, Russia, and Poland. In 2017, he was named International Superintendent of the Year. Another of our teammates, Greg Rhodes, is a federal prosecutor who was named the Deputy Chief of the Organized Crime and Drug Enforcement Task Force, overseeing ten federal prosecutors. Five of the seven seniors on our 1966-67 team went into education as teachers and coaches. Dr. Mike Devine retired as the Director of the Truman Library in Independence, Missouri in 2014. Previously, he had served as the Illinois State Historian and the Director of the Illinois State Historical Society. For several years, he was a professor at the University of Wyoming. Successes such as these, both on and off the court, are far from average. While I was at Loras, we joked that the school's slogan should be "Send Loras a boy, and we'll send you a man." A couple of the guys I went to school with serve to prove that statement was true. Greg Gumbel, 1967, an English major like me, is one of the top sportscasters on TV. We played on the same intramural football team and lived next door to each other as sophomores. Tom Miller, 1966, Harvard Law School 1969, became Iowa's Attorney General. First elected in 1978, he is now the longest serving state AG in the nation. Mike Blouin, 1966, started as an elementary teacher, and then was elected to the Iowa House of Representatives, then Iowa Senate, then Iowa Representative in U.S. Congress. Bill Bolster, class of 1967, became President and CEO of CNBC. Nothing average about those guys.

CHAPTER
TWELVE

When I played basketball in college, I would be so psyched up before a game, so intense, that I nearly became another person. I was aggressive, physical, and downright belligerent. I was mentally wound so tightly I was ready to kick ass if necessary to win. So much so, that on three occasions I was involved in fights breaking out on the court. Sadly, I started all three.

It happened twice my sophomore season, and both times it was against the same player. He was much shorter than I, about 6'2", and to compensate for the physical disadvantage, he was constantly pulling, holding, pushing, pinching. I finally snapped and punched him. Before he could retaliate, someone grabbed him from behind and began to pull him back. With both of his arms pinned to his side, I punched him again. Both benches emptied, and there were lots of pushing and shoving. Both of us were ejected from the game. Back in those days, fights weren't terribly uncommon, due in part to the fact that there was no carryover punishment or suspension. We probably had three or four fights each year. I was eligible to play the next game.

When we played that same team later in the year, the same thing happened--the pushing, holding, pulling. Once again, the same player and

I got into a fight in the middle of the game. We played them twice a year for the next two years, and it was always tense between the two of us, but no fisticuffs were involved again.

The most embarrassing incident occurred my senior year. We were playing a team in our home gym, and although I hadn't started, I was in the game fairly early. One of their best players was a guy about my size, and I was guarding him. He was off to a good start and had already scored eight or ten points. I had a single basket. We were mixing it up pretty well in the lane area: elbows, hips, jostling--the usual "big man" stuff on both offense and defense. I don't recall now (fifty years later) exactly what happened, but I snapped and punched him in the face. He was surprised and swung back but missed. I was in a rage and plowed forward and got in two more shots before our teammates and the referees separated us. Again, we were both ejected. His absence probably hurt his team more than mine did, and we went on to win the game.

Although this incident was embarrassing at the time, my chagrin increased the following year. Both of us were coaching high-school basketball in northwest Iowa. At the end of the season, some civic group had a big banquet for area teams and coaches. We were both there with our respective teams. The coach of a nearby college was the featured speaker. It was the same school I'd had the fight with their top player. The college coach proceeded to tell the whole story of the brawl and our involvement. My opponent's team was staring at him in disbelief. My players were staring at me in disbelief. A year after the fact, we were both exposed as "do what I say, not what I do" kind of guys. So much for being a role model. I felt terrible, and I'm sure he did, also. These are stories I have rarely mentioned in the past fifty years, but I guess it goes to show my intense competitiveness and desire to win.

CHAPTER

THIRTEEN

Coach Jerry Potts had been a high school basketball coach in northwest Iowa before becoming a coach at Loras our junior year. He was the freshman team coach, but when Coach Zahren suddenly resigned, Coach Potts took over, and was later named head coach. As a high- school coach, he had made many contacts in the northwest Iowa area. One of them, Father Tom Gehlen, needed an English teacher and coach, so Father Tom asked Coach Potts if he had anyone on the team that could fill the bill. Another guy, Tom Derouin, and I were both English majors and played basketball. Tom also played tennis and is in the Loras Hall of Fame for his tennis skills and stellar record. He had also just been offered a job at Moline High School, which he accepted. He went on to be the state Tennis Coach of the Year (1992), coach of state champions (1992 & 1993), and National High School Athletic Coaches Association Coach of the Year (1994).

Coach Potts recommended me to Father Gehlen, and I accepted the offer to teach English 9, 10, 11, 12, speech, and study hall, at Immaculate Conception High School in Cherokee, Iowa. My duties also included serving as assistant basketball coach, assistant track coach, and head golf coach for the amazing total sum of $6,000 per year. Actually, as ridiculously low as that salary seems for my job responsibilities, it was about 95% of what the public school paid. It was a different time. Gas in 1967 was about twenty-five cents a gallon, and a burger at McDonald's was about fifteen cents, so that salary wasn't as outrageously low as it seems today.

Cherokee is located in the northwest corner of Iowa, about sixty miles from Sioux City. At that time, it was about 7,000 people. I.C. High School was 100 students for all four grades. Very small. I loved my time at I.C. The kids were great, and the staff was open and welcoming. We had a lot of after-game parties. I was young, had just turned twenty-two a couple of weeks before school started, and single. After a couple of weeks of school, one of the nuns came to me and said, "Mr. Riney, I'd like to speak with you after school. It's a very confidential matter." I said I'd see her and then spent the rest of the day wondering what in the world she wanted to talk with me about. Confidential? No idea.

At the end of the day, I went to her room, and she asked me to come in and to close the door. She then quietly asked, "Can I ask you to do me a favor? But you can't tell anyone about it." I nodded and said, "Sure, what is it?" She replied, "I'd like you to buy me a six pack of Schlitz beer. Put it in a brown paper bag and leave it on the back steps of the convent. Can you do that every Friday?" Stunned, I agreed to her request and followed her wishes on Friday the rest of the school year. Years later I realized what a double standard there was. The priests openly smoked and drank, but the nuns had to sneak a beer in the convent. Not fair. I've often wondered why she selected me and if I should be complimented or insulted.

FOURTEEN

While in Cherokee, I played on a "semi-pro" basketball team. In those days, NBA players weren't eligible to play on the American team in the Olympics. College players, AAU players, and Armed Forces players were the ones selected. I was blessed to play at the highest level beneath the NBA which was on the Army team and on two different AAU championship level teams. Not average. There were numerous other "semi-pro" teams sponsored by industry with many opportunities to play in games and tournaments. As mentioned, the competition in AAU ball was intense and at a very high level. On our team were two guys who had played at Yankton College in South Dakota. There was a guy named Dennis Walljasper, a 6'5" former Notre Dame player, who is in the Iowa Basketball Hall of Fame from his exploits at St. Mary's High School in Iowa City, Iowa. There was a guy who'd played at Augustana in South Dakota, and several others as well. We were pretty good and even beat the team who won the Iowa State AAU Championship which was considered quite a feat at the time. A couple of the guys we played against included Don Ross, a 6'8" guy from Waterloo East who was a Parade All-American and played at Kansas. Another good player was 6'8" Tim Powers from Rock Island Alleman who played at Creighton University, scored over 1,000 points, and was drafted by the Philadelphia 76ers.

One of my proudest achievements was in the improvement I made as a free throw shooter. My senior year of high school I was terrible. I shot 44% from the free throw line. My field goal percentage was better than that. I worked hard at improving and was a decent shooter in college, shooting close to 70%. At Cherokee I continued to improve and won a trophy at a large AAU tournament for having the highest free throw percentage for the three-day tournament. I made 18 of 20 for 90%. The year I played in the Army, I shot slightly over 95%. I was the one who shot the technical foul shots for our team, and in Army ball there were plenty of technical fouls. Once again, above average.

One of the area high schools had a fund-raiser and contracted the Harlem Magicians, led by Marques Haynes, the former Harlem Globetrotter dribbling whiz. In a dispute over salary, Haynes had left the Globetrotters and formed his own similar squad. We put together an outstanding team of players, including me, from Buena Vista University, Westmar College, Yankton College, Augustana University, and several others. Before the game we decided we were NOT going to let them make us look foolish but play straight basketball as well as we could. We didn't want to be stooges like the Washington Generals for the Globetrotters. After their first couple of attempts, they backed off from their tricks and silliness, and both teams played a great game of straight basketball. With a couple of seconds left and our squad ahead by several points, they called timeout and one of their guys went to the scorer's bench and announced over the PA that we were one of the best teams they'd ever played.

In that game, I made the most amazing move/shot I've ever made playing basketball. It was on a fast-break, and the ball came to me. I drove toward the basket and got off a prodigious leap. From out of nowhere, one of their players appeared and knocked the ball loose from my shooting hand. While still in the air, I caught the ball with the other hand, shot, and scored. The guy who had partially blocked my shot looked at me in amazement as we ran down the court and said, "Damn, that was a hell of a play."

I was assistant varsity coach, and our I.C. team was conference champions finishing with a 16-3 record. My JV team somehow also managed a winning record. This was the 1967-68 school year, and the Vietnam war was in full swing. Early in 1968 I was called for my draft physical, and much to my surprise I received a medical deferment. If one was over 6'6", he was exempt from the draft. I had been unaware of this particular statute but was happy it applied to me.

The woman in charge of my draft board back home thought this rule was ridiculous. She sent me paperwork about every three or four weeks that required me to go to a doctor and be measured to verify that I was indeed over 6'6". However, that all changed in March of 1968 when Secretary of Defense Robert McNamara recommended, and it became law, that the height requirement be raised to 6'8". I received my draft notice soon after. The height issue had nothing to do with "being a big target"; it was mostly about clothing. Guys my size back then couldn't buy things off the shelf. The army also liked the symmetry of all the soldiers being between about 5'10" and 6'2".

The school appealed my draft notice, and I was granted an extension to finish teaching the school year. In August of 1968, I was to report to my local draft board to go to basic training at Fort Polk, Louisiana, which was a far cry from the temperate Midwest. It was hot. It was humid. It was awful. Just like Vietnam would be. In fact, the army combat infantry AIT (Advanced Infantry Training), known as Tiger Land, was located there because its temperature, humidity, swamps and bayous were all similar to those of Vietnam.

FIFTEEN

On the first day of basic training, I was called out and made a temporary platoon sergeant. I got sergeant's stripes to wear and even got a private room in the barracks. Definitely not average, right? There were four platoons in our basic training company, and each was about 35 men. Our company was about 50% reservists and National Guardsmen, most of whom were college graduates from the Chicago area. The other half was made up of young men from Mississippi, Alabama, Arkansas. There were a few "others" like me.

The order of eating at all our meals was determined by inspection results. Each day there was a latrine inspection, a barracks inspection, a bunk inspection, a foot locker inspection. The order of eating was based on the results of the inspections: platoon with best scores ate first and so on. In the entire eight weeks of training, my platoon did not eat last a grand total of once. What a bunch of lazy human beings. Per military protocol, as platoon sergeant I ate last, after all my men. That sometimes gave me 10-15 minutes to eat. At the end of basic training I was down to slightly less than 200 pounds, and I was always hungry.

In September of 1968, the war in Vietnam was in full swing. In 1968 there were 16,592 war related deaths. As a result of this high level of carnage, several of us in basic training were selected to serve as a military burial team to assist with the growing "overload" of military burials. I was selected as one of the six pall-bearers. There were seven chosen as the firing squad, one was a bugler, one of the drill sergeants, an OIC (officer in charge), and a bus driver. A total of seventeen men. One of the other pall bearers was a black kid who had played football at Grambling State University. The other sixteen of us were white.

We spent several hours each day for nearly a week practicing the procedures involved in a military funeral and burial—not just what to do, how to do it, and when to do it, but the sharp precision and being able to perform many things in unison. It was interesting, and the drill sergeant did an excellent job instilling in us the honor and importance of what we had been selected to do.

On the day of the funeral, our crew loaded onto an olive green "school bus" for the trip. We were wearing our freshly pressed Class A uniforms, with white gloves and our shoes were shined to a glossy sheen. We had learned that the deceased was a 19-year old African-American sergeant. We traveled north from Fort Polk on a nice four-lane highway. Eventually we exited onto a two-lane road, then a blacktop, then a gravel road, and finally a dirt road. Man, we were in the middle of nowhere. We proceeded to a small, white church in a clearing of the woods. Very picturesque setting.

The little church was packed, but the only white people there were those of us on the burial team. I vividly recall the ceremony and that the eulogy given by the black minister was powerful and insightful. It brought me to tears even though I had never known this young sergeant. After the funeral we loaded onto our bus and set out for Shreveport, where the burial was to take place.

When we arrived in Shreveport, we went to the "colored" cemetery for the conclusion of the funeral process. The minister gave a few remarks, and then the military ritual began. I was one of the flag-folders, and presented the folded flag to the drill sergeant who then gave it to the OIC who formally presented it to the deceased's mother who was naturally very distraught. The 21-gun volley was fired, and taps was played. Taps in that situation is so moving it can bring tears to anyone's eyes. At the end of the ceremony, the deceased soldier's mother stood up and literally threw herself onto the casket, sobbing and moaning hysterically for her lost son. I will never forget that moment. Far, far from anything average.

Our burial team was again loaded onto the bus and traveled into Shreveport to get something to eat before our journey back to Fort Polk. We stopped at a likely looking restaurant and began to get off the bus—sixteen white soldiers in uniform and one black soldier. Just as we approached the door a middle-aged white man came out and held up his hand in the classic "stop where you are" gesture. "Y'all can't come in here if you got that nigger with you," he proclaimed. Shocked, the OIC and drill sergeant got into a heated discussion with the man and he proceeded to point out a small decal on the window of the door proclaiming it to be a "private club." Since we weren't members of the club, he could legally refuse to allow us to enter. Welcome to Louisiana in 1968.

We had just come from helping to bury a young black man who had died in the service of his country, and this jerk was telling us we couldn't get food at his restaurant because one of us was black. I remember at the time noticing that our black comrade didn't seem to be as upset as the rest of us. Sadly, he was used to this type of discrimination, but for the rest of us it was a shocking insight into reality. In all my previous experiences, this was far from average.

Most of the physical and emotional stress in basic training was relatively easy for me. I was better at some things (I could walk all day) than at others (I hated running in formation). I know no reason why, but I really excelled at the pugil stick training. It simulates combat with a rifle fitted with a bayonet. At the end of a couple of weeks of training, we had a company-wide elimination tournament. I kicked butt and easily made the finals. My opponent in the company championship was a recruit who had played football at Arizona or Arizona State University. He was about 6'2" and 220 pounds.

In the introduction of our bout, the drill sergeant managed to whip the crowd of about 150 basic trainees into a frenzy. They formed a circle around us in the sand, screaming and yelling. He then said that since Private Riney was so much bigger (taller!) than my opponent, he would get to attack. So, I remained crouched in the middle of a circle of 150 screaming, rabid men while he came running at me full speed, screaming bloody murder. As he swung his stick at me, in a nanosecond I realized he was left-handed, so my move to block his attack was useless. Our sticks did not meet, and he hit me solidly on the side of my head. It was "goodnight, sweet prince," the only time I've ever been knocked unconscious in my life. I almost see stars again just remembering that blow.

At the end of basic training, there's a huge "graduation ceremony" where hundreds of soldiers will march past reviewing stands filled with commanding officers, parents, and families. The Commandant gives a speech, the band plays, and basic training ends. Prior to the ceremony, all of us in our company who were taller than 6'4" were pulled from the ranks and told to go to our barracks and wait until graduation was finished. The army didn't want us tall guys to screw up the symmetry of the ranks like stalks of corn growing in a soybean field.

After the ceremony, the drill sergeants passed out both the individual orders to each of us indicating where we would be going next and our MOS--military occupational specialty. Most of the guys were 11B, which is combat infantryman, and they went to the other side of the base for AIT (advanced infantry training) at dreaded Tiger Land. In its apparent reasonable logic, the army must have assumed that since I was a college graduate and had taught English for a year, I knew how to type. I didn't. Still don't. Never had a moment of typing instruction. But the army said I was a clerk typist, gave me fifteen days of leave, and assigned me to HQ, 8th Armored Squadron, 1st Air Cavalry in Fort Knox, Kentucky, just outside of Louisville.

SIXTEEN

When I arrived at Fort Knox, it was near the end of October 1968. Fort Knox was like a small city with a population of about 15,000 personnel. When I reported, they looked at me, looked at my 201 file and saw that I had played college basketball, and told me to go to Sadowski Field House to play basketball. I became a member of the squadron, or company team of ten or twelve members. A company normally has about 150-200 men. We played a couple of games each week for several weeks against other company teams. When the season ended, an "all-star" team of ten players was selected to play in the next level of competition--the battalion level. A battalion is about 1,000 men and each battalion had selected a team. Again, we played twice weekly for several weeks against other battalion teams. At the end of the season, an "all-star" team was again selected to play at the brigade level. A brigade consists of about 3,000-5,000 men. Brigade level basketball was super competitive. Most players had played in college, some in the pros. We played four nights each week for several weeks. When the season ended, another "all-star" team was selected to represent Fort Knox in competition against other fort teams. I was the only member of the 194th Brigade to make the Fort Knox team.

I became the company clerk whose primary duty was the daily "Morning Report." The Morning Report documented all personnel who were present, absent or missing. It listed who was on leave, who was in the infirmary and so on. In Army world, it was perhaps the most important document to be filed daily. I was then on orders to report for basketball practice at noon. As a way to provide entertainment for the troops, especially those in basic training, the various squadrons, battalions, brigades, had athletic teams made up of soldiers that played against each other. As previously mentioned, the "Crown Jewel" was the Fort Knox post team.

The Fort Knox post team was the best basketball team with which I've ever been associated. There were two guys from Bradley University, and one of them, Al Smith, went on to lead the ABA in assists while playing for the Denver Rockets. John Comeaux had played at Grambling State University and then in the ABL for the New Orleans Buccaneers. Mike Weaver, from Northwestern University, had been a two-time team MVP, was named All-Big Ten, and was drafted by the Chicago Bulls. He declined and went into the family business, Weaver Popcorn. We had a guy who had played at Colorado University, one from Seton Hall University, one from Detroit University,(now known as Detroit Mercy University) one from Murray State in Kentucky, one from Michigan State who had been a pitcher for the Los Angeles Dodgers, one from the College of Wooster in Ohio, Al Albers from Upper Iowa University against whom I had played for a couple of years in college, and me.

The teams we played against were equally loaded. Fort Campbell in Kentucky had Charlie Paulk who was the first-round draft pick of the Milwaukee Bucks and later was traded with Flynn Robinson, so the Bucks could get Oscar Robertson. Jerry Chambers played for Fort Dix in New Jersey. He had played for the University of Utah and was MVP of the 1966 NCAA Final Four. He was the first-round pick of the Lakers and was later involved in a three-player deal which brought Wilt Chamberlain to the Lakers.

One of our games to "entertain the troops" was against, you guessed it, the Harlem Magicians. The biggest compliment I've ever received about my basketball skills happened in that game. I had looked at the advertising poster before the game, and their record was something like 1,500-6. I was impressed because it included one more loss than when I had played against them a year earlier in Iowa. Early in the game during a free throw, one of their players stared at me and finally said, "You're that guy from that team in Iowa who beat us, aren't you? Man, that was a hell of a shot." I was stunned that a guy who played a couple of hundred games a year would remember me and a shot I had made. I'm confident that was not an average play.

The highlight of the season was the Basketball Championships of the First Army Area. That included all the Army posts east of the Mississippi River. It was held at Fort Meade, Maryland, in March of 1969. The tournament was divided into divisions based on the sizes of the Army bases. We were in the "big" division with bases like Fort Rucker (Alabama), Fort Campbell (Kentucky), Fort Dix (New Jersey), Fort Benning (Georgia), Fort Bragg (North Carolina), Fort Meade (Maryland), and a few more I've forgotten.

The format of the tournament was double elimination, and we won our first three games. That meant we practiced daily but didn't play as we waited for the remaining teams to eliminate themselves down to one team. It was an incredible week. After practice, we were free to do as we pleased. We saw quite a few of the bars and restaurants in the Baltimore-D.C. area. Team bonding, I think it was. One night about four or five of us spent hours at some place in Baltimore. We were drinking pitchers of beer and eating pizza like the world ended the next day. When we received our bill, it was over $400! At that time, my monthly take home salary was a grand total of $128. Thank God, the player who had been a pitcher in the LA Dodger organization paid the entire bill. Wish I could remember his name.

Our opponent in the finals was Fort Dix. They had one loss. We had none. So, if we won, we were champions. If they won, we played another game. After all the anticipation, we killed them. Our point guard, Al Smith, was the MVP of the tournament. We all received fancy watches with the First Army logo and the date and event. We flew back to Fort Knox where we were greeted like high-school state champions. We were driven all over the post in a firetruck, and later there was a huge banquet that was like a wedding reception: great food and open bar. The Commanding General gave a speech, and we all received an additional individual trophy about three feet tall. Letters of commendation from the commander, brigade commander, squadron commander, and unit commander were posted in our Army 201 file. That's actually a big deal in the military. I still have the letters and the watch, but somewhere along the line, the trophy disappeared.

I was still the company clerk for HQ, 8th Armored Squadron, 1st Air Cavalry. It was a good job, but now I was there all day--no more basketball practice at noon. We were the only Cavalry unit stateside, and most of the personnel were Vietnam veterans. Lots of helicopter pilots, mechanics, and door gunners. They were most definitely not an average group. I spent lots of time with three or four guys, and we became good friends. I also used to ride along on a helicopter whenever I had the opportunity. I loved it. Life was good. Then, in late May, I got orders assigning me to Vietnam. As was the standard procedure, I received a 30-day leave to go home, and then I was to report to Fort Lewis, Washington, to deploy to Vietnam. By now I was a Spec. 4 (Specialist Fourth Class), an E-4, or the equivalent of a corporal. My MOS (military occupational specialty) was now Personnel Specialist. I spent many hours wondering what the war and combat would be like. I'd heard so many "war stories" from the vets at Fort Knox. I wasn't scared, but I was certainly apprehensive. I was going unattached, not part of a unit, which meant I was going as an individual, so there was no chance of deducing in advance where I would be assigned.

SEVENTEEN

Vietnam. Every young man of draft age, civilian or soldier, spent hours wondering and worrying about Vietnam. I was no exception. I don't recall being afraid of dying, but I was filled with curiosity at how I would act. Would I be a coward? Would I run? Would I do my job? Thoughts like these were constantly in my mind.

I was to report to Fort Lewis, Washington. From my hometown of Keokuk, Iowa, that was no small logistical feat. I would take a bus to Burlington, Iowa, which was about an hour away. Then I transferred buses and went to Des Moines, and from there I flew to Seattle/Tacoma. Then it was Army transportation to Fort Lewis. This travel was a two-day ordeal, and I decided to wait a day before beginning my journey. I figured, "What the hell?" What they gonna do, send me to Vietnam?" I spent my "extra" night drinking and carousing with friends. The net result was that I arrived at Fort Lewis a day later than my orders stipulated. I also had not cut my hair during my thirty days of leave, so it was much too long by Army standards. I endured a severe ass-chewing from the NCO in charge for my tardiness and long hair, (immediately got a haircut), and went out to formation with hundreds, if not thousands, of young men waiting to go to Vietnam.

Men in green uniforms were milling about as far as the eye could see. Amazingly, I ran into a guy with whom I had gone to college, and after some small talk he asked me my MOS. When I told him, his face beamed, and he said, "Isn't it cool what happened yesterday?" (Yesterday--the day I was supposed to be there.) "What happened?" I wanted to know. "Everyone with that MOS was called out, and they told us we were having our orders changed. We're going to Germany instead of Vietnam!" I couldn't help but wonder if this was some kind of omen or sign for the future. However, since I hadn't been there, my orders were still for Vietnam. Being a day late and not getting re-routed to Germany was "above average" only in the sense I'd "done it my way."

The journey from Fort Lewis to Vietnam was long and arduous. As I recall, it was about sixteen hours. We flew to Hawaii and deplaned for an hour-and-a-half while the plane was refueled. At that time, so many were being sent to Vietnam the military alone could not keep up with the demand. As a result, most of those who went there went on commercial airlines. I don't remember what commercial airline we flew. From Hawaii, our plane went to the island of Guam. We refueled again but weren't allowed to get off the plane. Looking out the window, one could see rows and rows of B-52 bombers. Their power and beauty would be even more obvious to me in a few months. The last stage of the journey was to Cam Ranh Bay, Vietnam.

We arrived late in the evening, and after finding our duffle bags, we were loaded onto buses. These were just like school buses I'd spent so many hours on riding to games as a player and coach--with two major differences: these were olive drab green, and they had heavy wire over the windows (to keep grenades thrown at the buses from going inside). The heat and humidity were overpowering. Instantly we were all soaked with sweat. There were no air conditioners on the busses. It was difficult to imagine an entire year in that environment.

By the time we arrived at the replacement battalion, it was quite late and dark. There were literally hundreds of us, mostly all "newbies" like me. The area we were in was filled with long tables and benches. We sat down and began to organize our army records, including our 201 file which is the primary military record including date of induction, dates of promotions, test scores, MOS, and other pertinent information, such as dental records and medical records. From the time we had arrived, there was the sound of machine gun fire in the distance, and the sky looked like it was the 4th of July. I had no idea what was happening. Was that directed at us? Were those rockets? What the hell was going on? None of us had been issued weapons of any kind yet, so we were totally unarmed. As this sound of gunfire crescendo increased in volume, I noticed that none of the men who had started to process us were to be seen. So, there we sat, a couple hundred rookies, unarmed, not understanding what was happening, looking like deer in the headlights. After a couple of minutes, one of the processors came running out yelling, "We're under attack! Get to the bunkers."

Of course, we ran like hell to the bunkers. Cam Ranh Bay has the most beautiful beach I'd ever seen. But everything was on sand. So, in the bunkers we were sitting on sand. It was itchy and scratchy because it was so hot, and our adrenalin was making us sweat like we'd run a mile. We had no weapons, huddled together listening to the cacophony of sounds outside: the rattle of the machine guns, the explosions of rockets and mortars, small arms fire that seemed way too close for comfort, unexplained explosions that shook the earth. I don't honestly remember how long it lasted—many long minutes for sure. It certainly seemed like a lifetime. At some point, we were given the all-clear, and we came hesitatingly out of the bunkers. Wide-eyed and looking about, we returned to the procedure of "in processing."

When we were finally finished we were assigned to barracks. They were wooden buildings with concrete floors. The wooden walls were built with each slat on an angle, so the breeze could blow through and ventilate the building, and wire screen was on the inside of the walls. There were no air-conditioners. Outside the walls there were large barrels filled with sand and topped off with sandbags to give a modicum of protection from surprise rocket and mortar attacks. They had a tin roof. We were told that if more rockets came in during the night to grab our bunk's mattress and roll onto the floor and pull the mattress over us for cover. Twice more that night we had incoming rockets, so there wasn't a lot of sleep to be had. We spent too much time lying on the floor under the mattress, rather than sleeping on the mattress.

The next morning it was like watching a giant IMAX showing a Vietnam War movie. Across the bay, we could see the F-4 Phantoms dropping explosives and napalm. The F-4 is the plane that was used by both the Blue Angels and the Thunderbirds. It was highly mobile and super-fast, with a top speed of Mach 2.2. That's over 1,500 miles per hour. Cobra gunships rolled in, their mini-guns blasting with their distinctive groan. The Cobra was an attack helicopter capable of diving at speeds of over 200 mph. It was heavily armed with mini-guns and rockets. It was surreal to me: the noise, the view. I kept thinking, "I haven't been here twenty-four hours yet. How will I last a year?"

Later that day I was ok'd to go take a shower. The "shower" was about 100 yards away and consisted of a large water tank that was heated by the sun. There was a rope to pull, allowing water to cascade. I was wearing a pair of flip-flops I had brought with me and a green army towel. The towel was not large enough to go around me, so I was holding it together with one hand and carrying my shaving kit in the other. After the shower as I was ambling back to my barracks, we were hit once again with incoming rockets. I had about a fifty yard run to the nearest bunker. Running in flip-flops, holding a towel with one hand and a shaving kit with the other, is not the fast way to run. When I dived into the bunker, I was clad in only one flip-flop. Yep, naked as a jaybird, covered with sand, sweating from the heat, the exertion, and the adrenalin. As I lay there listening to the explosions, the one thought running through my mind was, "They're going to find my dead, naked body with all this sand in my butt." (Amatuer psychiatrists, feel free to analyze that.) I was certain after that incident that I'd never make it the entire year. Obviously, that turned out to be an incorrect conclusion.

We later learned many of the details of the attack. A little after midnight a barrage of 107 mm rockets soared across the bay and hit the air base. 107mm rockets were bad but not like the big 122mm rockets I later learned to fear. At the same time a small group of sappers cut through the perimeter wire and stormed through the compound, throwing satchel charges into buildings as they passed. Sappers were elite troops much like our

Rangers. They were highly trained in map reading, orienteering, breaching of obstacles and booby trap removal, explosives and demolitions. The purpose of sappers was to penetrate an American defensive perimeter in advance of a ground attack. This would cause American troops to fight in two directions at the same time. When penetrating a defensive perimeter, they would be naked. This prevented them from being entangled or slowed by their clothing getting snagged on barbed wire which was usually strung around US positions. Sappers were one of the greatest fears.

The 6th Convalescent Center is located next to the replacement battalion where I arrived. It's a place where wounded soldiers came to recuperate, relax, and forget the war for a period. The beach at Cam Ranh Bay is amazing: beautiful white sand and transparent waves rolling rhythmically into shore. A truly gorgeous place. That was all changed that night.

When it was all over, 100 patients and staff members of the convalescent center were wounded or killed. In all, the sappers hit 19 of the 94 buildings in the compound and four of them were totally destroyed.

CHAPTER
EIGHTEEN

Despite what the first day was like, I knew Cam Ranh Bay was normally one of the safer areas in Vietnam. So, I was happy to stay there as long as possible. The second full day there we had our morning formation after breakfast, and we were informed that we would all be undergoing testing--three hundred of us sitting in row after row of picnic-like tables, taking army tests. Many of the men simply blew it off, but I treated it like it was life and death. I concentrated on each and every question. The next day about half of our group were called out and told they were going to 1st Infantry, or the 82nd Airborne, or some other unit. The rest of us, about 150 guys, had more tests. Once again, I focused like a wild man. The next day, the same thing occurred: about half again were assigned to various units throughout Vietnam. Those of us remaining had more tests. This went on for several days until there were only about a dozen of us remaining.

Another guy and I were called out and told we would be going to Da Nang. We collected our gear, boarded the aircraft, and off we went. I've never heard of anything like it in the Army, because when we arrived in Da Nang, we went through a job interview. I swear to God. I have no recollection what the job was after all these years, but it's the only time I ever heard that the Army didn't just tell us where to go. The other guy was selected, and he stayed in Da Nang. I have no idea what criteria they used. He did have a master's degree from Northwestern University, so perhaps that was the deciding factor. I still have no idea.

I was then flown to Tan Son Nhut airbase outside Saigon and taken to Long Bien Post where I was assigned to HQ, 1st Logistical Command. 1st Log was the largest command in Vietnam with over 50,000 men spread out over the entire country. Almost every piece of Army equipment sent to Vietnam was processed, transported, issued, and maintained by the 1st Log. Not only was 1st Log responsible for providing the Army troops with the basic weapons of war, but it also clothed and fed them and supplied them with virtually every amenity.

I was assigned to Security, Plans, and Operations (SPO), the Force Development and Training section. We worked in a building that was air-conditioned because there were computers there--the big old-fashioned kind with reels about two feet in diameter. They were giant machines, looking nothing like the computers of today. My job had nothing to do with them, but I enjoyed the cool temperature. The computers were used to help keep track of the over 700,000 tons of supplies each month.

About the second week of my time there as I stepped onto the shuttle bus which transported us from our hootches (barracks) where we lived to the complex where we worked, I noticed a guy staring at me. It was Joe Heiple, my roommate from freshman year of college. I hadn't seen him in six years. He had already been there a couple of months and was assigned to HQ, USARV (Headquarters, United States Army Republic of Vietnan), another military anacronym) to which I was later transferred. We were together for about ten months before he went home. Although he served before I was there, my other college roommate, Joe Hajek, is also a Vietnam vet, and his hootchmate was Pat Sajek--yes, that one on "Wheel of Fortune."

Long Bien Post was huge, with a peak of about 60,000 personnel. If one had to be in Vietnam, it was one of the best places to be. It was reasonably safe, with little to no danger of being ambushed or dealing with booby traps inside the compound itself, or "inside the wire" as we said. Although that's what everyone thought about Cam Ranh Bay too. Unfortunately, we had an exceptionally large number of senior officers: generals, colonels, and such. In fact, General Creighton Abrams had an office in our complex at USARV. I was once involved in a briefing for him, which was very intense and high-pressure. With all the high-ranking personnel on base, we got more than our share of rockets and even mortars fired at us. We were most commonly hit with 122 mm rockets. A 122 mm rocket is 6 feet long with a TNT head. They're able to fly up to 17 miles or so. They are both spin, and fin stabilized and can be fired from specifically designed tubes or placed against an object like a log. They aren't especially accurate but are capable of doing immense damage. They could be set to explode as an airburst, set for delayed explosion, or set to dig in several feet before exploding. If you were the enemy, would you rather kill an unknown private or a general? Sometimes not being average has its drawbacks.

I myself was later assigned to HQ, USARV (Headquarters, United States Army in Vietnam). USARV controlled the activities of all US Army service and logistical units in South Vietnam. USARV controlled ten major support commands in Vietnam, and also supervised 71 smaller units. Some of the units included 1st Logistical Command, 1st Aviation Brigade, 44th Medical Brigade, 525th Military Intelligence Group, 18th Military Police Brigade, U.S. Army Security Agency Group, and U.S. Army Engineer Command. I was again with the SPO (Security, Plans, and Operations) shop, and the Force Development and Training section. Everything we did was classified. Our file cabinets were safes with a combination lock and incendiary devices inside in the unlikely case that we were overrun by the enemy. We had to take outdated material and extra copies to the burn bin every day because everything was classified. The hub of the system was the LOCC (Logistical Operations Control Center). Entrance to this room was permitted only to those on the entry list of personnel, which I was. The entry list was comprised of those with a "need to know" based on one's job, not the rank of the personnel. Two armed guards sat outside the entry, in addition to the armed guards stationed at all the entrances to the building itself.

One wall of the LOCC contained floor-to-ceiling maps of all four of the military divisions in Vietnam: I Corps, II Corps, III Corps, and IV Corps. Push-pins indicated the locations of our units and those of the enemy, both

NINETEEN

I served in Vietnam from August 1969 to August 1970. Even though the Vietnam war was ended in April of 1975, we were already working primarily on the massive turn-over of Army equipment to the ARVNs (Army of the Republic of Vietnam—the people we were there to help). We were reviewing the Army Table of Organization and Equipment (TOE or TO&E) for all the units which were to be turned over to the South Vietnamese, so they could fight their own war. A detailed listing of specific organization, staffing, and equipment of units is obviously classified information. This process was code-named "Project Buddy." Later, when the actual turn-over began, it was known as "Operation Buddy."

We normally worked from 7:00 AM until about 7:00 PM on most days. Sundays were usually more relaxed. There was another guy who did my job from 7:00 PM until 7:00 AM. The nature of the job required me to periodically be out and about. I was frequently in Saigon getting or delivering data. That's where MACV (Military Assistance Command Vietnam) was located. MACV was the headquarters for all the countries helping fight on our side. Many people don't realize that South Korea, Australia, New Zealand, and several others were actually involved in fighting the Viet Cong and North Vietnamese along with us. On several occasions I went to DiAn, (pronounced Zee Ann) about 12 miles from Saigon, which was the base of the famous 1st Infantry Division, known as "The Big Red One." They were the last unit to leave Vietnam in 1975, and those guys saw the real shit, more combat than one can imagine. The Big Red One had 17 Medal of Honor winners and over 20,000 casualties. There were other little villages and fire bases, most of whose names I never knew, to which we also went. As a carryover from my days with the 1st Cavalry at Fort Knox, when I had some free time, I used to ride along on helicopters "for fun." In retrospect, that was pretty stupid. No idea why I would put myself in unnecessary jeopardy. Not above average.

Our unit had a section of the Long Bien perimeter to man and guard. There were bunkers about every 100 yards. From dusk to dawn there were four men with their rifles in each bunker. There were thousands of rounds of ammo, an M-60 machine gun with thousands of belted rounds, and an M-79 grenade launcher and many rounds for it. Claymore mines were to the front, with interlocking fields of fire. Each was marked with a small X on the back with phosphorescent paint. The VC (Viet Cong) were known to sneak up, turn the claymores around, then back away and be seen. When the claymores were set off, they discharged *at the soldiers*, not at the VC, hence the painted X to be sure the claymores were pointing in the proper direction. Concertina wire coils helped to protect the area directly in front of the bunker also. Randomly throughout the concertina, we wired empty beer and pop cans with a couple of rocks inside. If the VC tried to sneak through the wire, they most likely would cause the cans to shake, making a tell-tale noise. Outside the wire was "Charlie," the Viet Cong, known as Victor Charlie, or simply Charlie. And from day one we were trained to always remember that "Charlie owns the night."

Our most dangerous opponent while on guard duty was mosquitos. They were huge and aggressive. We virtually bathed in bug repellant every time it was our turn for guard duty. Army bug repellant was effective-to a point-but it had a pungent odor. Our section of the perimeter suffered from occasional sniper attacks. Because of the defoliant Agent Orange, there wasn't much cover for them. Thus, the snipers were forced to fire from quite a distance which meant they weren't very accurate. It was still good for high blood pressure and an adrenaline boost.

As I was going through the familiarization program when I first arrived in-country, which involved qualifying on the M-60 machine gun and the M-79 grenade launcher, I was amazingly good with the M-79. I have no idea why, much like my earlier skill with the pugil sticks. M-79s can shoot about 400 yards. We had a target range set up with old trucks, Jeeps, tanks, and armored personnel carriers at various distances. I was awesome. The instructor would say to hit the tank, and I'd somehow calculate the distance, set the sight and fire. Boom, direct hit. This happened over and over. No explanation as to why I was able to do this. I began to think I was too good and might be getting myself an MOS change to 11 Bravo, combat infantryman. Thank God that didn't happen. Beating through the bush everyday wasn't a high priority for me.

At daybreak, two of the men in the bunker would be picked up and shuttled back to the rear, and two would remain until the new shift arrived at dusk. That long daytime shift from dawn to dusk was unique. If someone you knew well was your partner, it was a time of long, deep, conversations--usually about what was going to happen when you returned to the world. If your partner was someone you weren't familiar with, it was an excellent chance to get to know each other.

Smaller bunkers with no munitions were located between the main bunkers and were manned by two soldiers when the perimeter was under attack. Much of the vegetation in front of and around the bunker areas had been destroyed by the chemical defoliant Agent Orange to provide a better view and clearer field of fire. It was comforting to realize there was less likelihood that Charlie would be able to sneak up on us. Little did I realize the impact Agent Orange would have on me and many of my colleagues later in life.

Our unit's rotation was to be on guard duty about every second or third day. During the time of Tet, the Vietnamese New Year, and after the 1968 Tet Offensive, our unit went on daily patrols outside the perimeter since enemy activity was much increased.

The same men did not go out every day on patrol as the groups were rotated, so different men were exposed daily. For us non-infantry types, those patrols certainly raised one's blood pressure and pulse rate. I remember being on patrol and coming upon a small stream. My natural inclination was to look for a way around it. Nope, one was to continue on the assigned route, which meant going straight ahead through the thigh-deep water. Those patrols helped to remind us what the "real war" out in the boonies was like day after day for many of our comrades. During the Tet Offensive in 1968, the VC had breached the perimeter in the section our unit was assigned. They over ran the area and did considerable damage within the actual compound. That's why we had to go out on patrol during the time of Tet in 1969 too.

CHAPTER

TWENTY

I doubt that I would have ever volunteered to go to Vietnam. However, part of me is glad that I did end up there. I'm sure that had I not gone, I would have always wondered what it was like, and if I would have measured up when under life-and-death circumstances. I did do the job I was assigned to do to the best of my abilities. Thanks to my coaches, Uncle Tuck, and my parents, I did what had to be done as well as I could do it. "Good enough" isn't acceptable when a task should be done right, especially when someone's life is involved. My reward was the feeling of doing the right thing well, because other people's lives were in the balance. It was a good sensation and mentally stimulating, although I didn't think about it in those terms at the time.

My tangible reward from the Army for doing a good job was being awarded a Bronze Star medal and several less prestigious awards. The Bronze Star is the nation's 4th highest award following the Congressional Medal of Honor, the Distinguished Service Cross, and the Silver Star. Like many Vietnam veterans, upon returning to the States, I kept a low profile about my service in Vietnam. The country was divided about that war and its warriors. Generally speaking, we vets were not welcomed home, nor were we thanked for our service. Many of my friends, colleagues, and students were unaware until the past dozen years or so that I was a Vietnam vet. In general, I think society now can hate the war without hating the warrior. As I grow older, I have become much prouder of my service there and any recognition I may have earned.

If we recall all the humorous Army characters on TV and in the movies, many are men who know someone who knows someone who owes them a favor. Remember Sgt. Bilko and Radar O'Reilly? In the real Army, that's how it goes, too. The nature of my work put me in position to know many guys who could pull a string here or there. I was also one who might be able to help someone else out down the road. If it weren't for guys owing other guys "favors," I don't know how the Army would have been able to get anything done. For example, any soldier was eligible to go to Vung Tau, Vietnam, for a three day "in-country" R & R. Several buddies and I knew the manifest clerk, so we were able to go for four days. Vung Tau was a beautiful place: great beach, crystal clear water, everything one would want for a brief vacation. Similarly, an R & R to another country was normal. Since I "knew some guys," I spent the first week of July in Bangkok, Thailand, and the last week of July in Hong Kong. I returned in time for my DEROS (Date Eligible to Return from Over Seas) on August 7, 1970.

My return to the "real world" began at the 90th Replacement Battalion on the edge of Long Bien post. Our flight, a commercial one, left Vietnam and flew to Guam to refuel. Again, we sat on the plane. Then it was on to Hawaii, and like on the way to Vietnam, we deplaned and spent about an hour-and-a-half in the airport. I jokingly tell people I've been to Hawaii twice. After boarding again, the last leg took us to the Replacement Company in San Francisco. After a few hours of paperwork, receiving new uniforms (since we were wearing tropical uniforms we'd had for a year), and getting haircuts, those of us like me were out of the Army and free to begin a new life back in the world. It was August 7, 1970. At that time, it was common for soldiers returning from Vietnam to be "attacked" by "hippies," and some were spit upon and called names such as "baby killer" and such. That never happened to me. At the risk of being arrogant, I was

25 years old, 6'7" and 240 pounds, in shape, and had just spent a year in Vietnam. Had that happened, I'd probably just be out of prison by now.

I flew to Chicago, and a woman I had dated before going overseas met me at O'Hare. I went with her to her hometown of Rockford, Illinois, for several days. I was introduced to her family and friends. We continued to date afterwards, and the next August, we were married. That was my first wife, Laura.

I then flew from Rockford to Quincy, Illinois, and my sister, Becky, picked me up at the airport, and we drove the hour to my hometown of Keokuk, Iowa. My problem was that the little Catholic school in Cherokee, Iowa, at which I had taught before being drafted into the Army no longer existed. It had closed due to declining enrollment. I had no job. While in Vietnam I had applied to and been accepted at graduate school at the University of Iowa, so I decided to go.

TWENTY-ONE

My time in Iowa City was once again dominated with basketball. I played in lots of pick-up games at the fieldhouse at the University that fall, including some that involved Iowa Hawkeye players. It was fun, and I usually played pretty damn well. I remember the first time I actually played on the game court for the Hawkeyes. It was surreal. Yet, the first time I ever felt old was that fall. I was shooting baskets all by myself in the Iowa Fieldhouse which had about eight basketball courts in addition to the game court when the bleachers were pushed back. I loved being there playing on the Hawkeye's court. The aroma of popcorn hung in the air, and in my mind, I could hear the roar of the crown when the Hawkeyes were playing. As a youngster I had attended many games there, and it was a thrill to be there even if it was simply shooting around.

I noticed another guy shooting alone on a court several courts over. We were about the only two guys there in the middle of the afternoon, so I went over to where he was, and we began to shoot together. I couldn't help but notice this dude was really tall. He dwarfed me. As we talked and shot, I asked him his name. "Kevin Kunnert," he responded. I then realized he was Iowa's seven-foot center who was from Dubuque. Kevin was a cousin of Fred Kunnert with whom I had played at Loras. "What's your name?" he asked. "Charley Riney" I replied. "Oh, my God," he said. "I used to go watch you play at Loras when I was a little kid." Ouch. Little kid? Kevin went on to lead the Big Ten Conference in rebounding for three years, was the Iowa team MVP twice, earned All-American honors, was a first-round draft pick in the NBA, and played for nine years in the league.

When basketball season officially began in mid-October, I was surprised to be asked to play on a team known as Red's World. Red's World was a men's haircut and grooming place in downtown Iowa City. Red, the owner, loved basketball and sponsored a team which played in the city league and traveled about to play in AAU tournaments. Chad Calabria and Glen Vidnovic, both from Iowa's undefeated Big Ten championship team of 1970, and both All-Big Ten, were the headliners. They were both drafted into the NBA, Chad by the Phoenix Suns, and Glen by the Cleveland Cavaliers, but neither made the final cuts of their draft teams. Other players included a guy who had played at Notre Dame, several Iowa football players who were superb basketball players, and yours truly, Charley Riney--once again, no place for average players. Primarily because Chad and Glen had played for the Hawkeyes, we scrimmaged against the Iowa freshman team several times. Once again, it was a thrill to actually be playing on the Iowa court—and against the Hawkeyes, even if they were only the freshmen team. We were undefeated in the city league which was a tough league with numerous former college players involved. Next, we played in the Iowa state AAU championship tournament in Marshalltown. We won that easily and moved on to the national tournament where we lost to a team consisting of players from Kansas University.

Academically I was in the educational psychology department pursuing a degree in secondary school counseling. My intention was to become a high school guidance counselor. I attended the 1970-71 school year plus summer school. That gave me 32 hours toward the 38 hours required. In August of 1971, Laura and I were married and moved to Beloit, Wisconsin. She began teaching elementary school, and I started coaching and teaching English at Beloit Catholic High School. I was assistant football coach, freshman basketball coach, and head track coach. Not an average workload.

CHAPTER

TWENTY-TWO

Our football team won the conference, but the real highlight was defeating Marengo High School and stopping their state record 45-game winning streak. My freshman basketball team had a nice season, winning most of their games. Track season was unbelievable.

The kids I had in track were quite possibly the most amazing and talented group of athletes with which I've ever been associated. We were undefeated in every meet we entered and easily won both the conference championship and the state championship. Those guys were unbelievable. There were three who threw the shot over 50 feet, and three who long-jumped over 20 feet. I had a 6'1" and a 6'4" high-jumper. We had a 4:18.2 miler and 1:57.6 half-miler. Our mile relay team ran 3:27.8. Most amazing was this: a young man named Addison Riley had placed 6th in the state meet 2-mile the year before. He came to me and said he wanted to try the hurdles. He was about 6'3", 185 pounds, and tough as hell. So, we tried the hurdles. He was undefeated for the season in the highs and lows; he was even state champ in both, with a best of 14.7 seconds in the high hurdles. The next year he was again state champion in the high hurdles. These performances were in 1972 and would still be ultra-competitive today. The next year our team lost a couple of meets during the season but won the conference meet and were state champions again. In those two seasons, we had eleven individual state champions and twice won the state mile relay. In addition, we won thirteen medals of 2nd to 5th place. The Hanson twins, Jim and Joe, were incredible. Both later ran at UW-LaCrosse, and each was a nine-time All-American in cross-country, indoor track, and outdoor track. Both are in the UW-LaCrosse Hall of Fame and the NAIA (National Association of Intercollegiate Athletics) Hall of Fame.

Perhaps the highlight of the season was competing against Beloit Memorial High School in a dual meet. Memorial was about five times as large as Beloit Catholic and a state power in their own right. The Rockford newspaper covered the competition and stated that the size of the crowd was 1,000. That's unbelievable for a high school dual track meet. They won the meet, but we won several of the "glamour" events. In the quarter mile, our sophomore, Mike Borgerding, nipped Beloit Memorial's senior Jim Caldwell for the win. Caldwell went on to play football at the University of Iowa where he was a four-year starter as defensive back and became a very successful coach, both in college and the NFL. He's the same Jim Caldwell who coached Indianapolis to the Super Bowl after Tony Dungy retired. Most recently he was head coach of the Detroit Lions.

The second year at Beloit Catholic, I was named head basketball coach in addition to my other teaching and coaching duties. We had a decent team and finished third in the conference. We came on great at the end of the season and made it to the Elite Eight of the state tournament. We were eliminated, but it was a fantastic experience. We were assigned to use the Milwaukee Bucks's locker room for our first game at state. That alone was the highlight for most of my squad. While I was head coach in track for two years, our team had won two state championships. While I was head basketball coach for one season, we'd made it to state. Certainly not average performances. At the time, I thought, "What's the big deal about winning state championships, or qualifying for state?" Boy was I naïve. In the next forty-two years, I was fortunate to coach a basketball team to the Sweet Sixteen in Illinois once. I can appreciate the significance of the earlier accomplishments much more, now that I realize the difficulty involved. Most coaches never have even a single team make it to state or win a state championship.

CHAPTER

TWENTY-THREE

My second heart attack was in June of 2006, nearly six years to the day after my first one. School was out for the summer, and I had slept late and gone to a local restaurant for a late breakfast. I had leisurely eaten my bacon, eggs, wheat toast, and coffee while reading the morning's newspaper. Life was good. I still suffered heartburn from time to time, and as I drove home, thinking about my plans to mow the lawn, heartburn-like pain began in my chest. I wasn't particularly concerned.

By the time I arrived at home, my old friend the sumo wrestler had returned to sit on my chest. I went inside, sat down, and began sweating profusely. The pain in my chest continued to increase. I decided this situation was more than simple heartburn. Just like my first attack, chest pain was the only symptom I experienced--no nausea, no vomiting, no shortness of breath-- just horrible, intense chest pain.

I sat there thinking, "Should I drive myself to the hospital [about 15 minutes away], or should I call 911?" Since Fran was at work, I was home alone. As the pain became even more intense, and the sweat was now literally running down my face, I decided to call 911. After calling 911, an ambulance arrived in a few minutes, and I was placed on a stretcher and put in the vehicle. Immediately, I was hooked up to an IV and an EKG machine. My decision to call 911 was a good one. Had I tried to drive myself I would have had to pull over due to the pain, or more probably, I would have had an accident.

Much like my first heart attack visit to the emergency room, a large group of nurses, technicians, and doctors began assisting me immediately. As before, I was soon in the catheter lab and having an angiogram. When the procedure was completed, the doctor explained that what had happened to me was rare. In layman's language, a blockage had begun to form "downstream" from the previously inserted stent area. As a result, the slower speed of the bloodstream in that area had allowed a blockage to form in the stent itself. Once again, I had a 90% blockage of my old nemesis, the widow-maker.

The plan was to go in and unblock the clot and insert yet another stent. I don't honestly recall if the new stent was installed next to the existing stent or inside it. In any case, the procedure was performed successfully, and in a day or two I was home. Placing a stent has become such a commonplace procedure today in the world of cardiac surgery; it's truly amazing.

A week or so later, I was back at the cardio rehab center. Once again, the sessions were three days a week for an hour or so. As before, the rehab staff carefully monitored blood pressure, heart rate, and blood sugar before, during, and after the workout. I spent time on the treadmill, the rower, and a stationary bike; I also had some resistance work with light weights and rubber resistance bands. It was a comprehensive workout, and I made good progress. Within a couple of weeks, I felt as good as new.

As had happened after my first heart attack, I spent lots of time wondering why I was the exception to the rule. I remembered that 90% fatality rate of the widow-maker, yet now I had twice survived. My "above-average philosophy" I'd somewhat adapted from my friend helped. It's not that I feel superior to, or better than others. It's more of a feeling of "I got this. Bring it on. I can handle whatever there is to be handled." In my mind, I can overcome whatever hurdle gets in the way. I have before, and I will again. I did it in school, in basketball as a player, as a track athlete, as a soldier, as a coach, as a businessman, and as a teacher. I'm not average. I've got this!

CHAPTER

TWENTY-FOUR

When school began again in mid-August of 2012, most of the students and other teachers were unaware that I'd had a heart attack a couple of months earlier. I was feeling fine, working out several days a week, watching my diet, and generally living the good life. It didn't take long for me to basically forget I'd had two heart attacks, both involving the "widow-maker." My life was normal, and there were no restrictions of significance placed upon me. I was teaching three classes every day at South Beloit High school and also working as a part-time real estate broker. I had retired from full-time teaching and begun to collect my Teachers Retirement Service pension. Under Illinois law, I was allowed to teach up to 500 hours a year and not jeopardize my teacher's pension, so I was compelled to take several "sick" days to stay under the state's limit. I jokingly told people that "now that I've retired, I'm down to two jobs."

My time at South Beloit was enjoyable: excellent administration, great colleagues, and students who were attentive. What more could a teacher ask for? I truly enjoyed those ten years.

In January of 2016, I began to notice that if I exerted myself, like running back upstairs because I'd forgotten to put on my watch, I was pitifully short of breath. A single flight of stairs had me breathing like I'd run a quarter-mile. It was painful, but I'd sit down and breathe slowly and deeply, and in forty-five seconds or a minute, I was fine. It didn't feel like my two previous heart attacks; it felt more like a problem with my lungs. Once again, I had no other heart attack symptoms, just pain in my chest, but it felt different than the "heart burn" I'd had previously.

As time passed, this shortness of breath occurred with increasing frequently. I also noticed that it required less and less exertion to cause this problem. Over several months, I realized it was happening several times daily. I would simply sit down, breathe slowly and deeply, and I would feel normal again. I had a regularly scheduled appointment with my primary care physician coming up on June 6, 2016, so I just waited, planning to speak with her at that time.

I had spent the last week of May visiting my sister and her husband on Sanibel Island, Florida. One night those symptoms occurred again. This time was different, however, because the pain didn't go away as usual. It lasted for several hours. I was nearly hyperventilating after all the deep, slow, breaths I'd done during most of the night. I began to think that this was indeed something serious.

I returned from my time in Florida, and on June 6th, went to my doctor's appointment. I had never changed my doctor from the time when I had lived in Byron, Illinois, so I drove to the clinic in Byron. When I was led to the examination room, after a short time in the waiting room, I asked the nurse if they wanted a urine specimen. She checked her material and said they didn't need one this time. I told her I needed to go to the bathroom then, since I'd been "saving" in case they wanted one.

The restroom was on the other side of the clinic, and I tried to go as fast as I could because I imagined the doctor and nurse waiting impatiently back in the room. I "power-walked" to get back to the exam room and was surprised to find no one waiting there. I was indeed breathing like I'd run a mile, so I sat down and began to breathe deeply and slowly. At that moment the doctor entered. She asked me what the trouble was, and I explained what had been happening the past six months or so. Within minutes I was hooked up to the EKG machine and soon found myself in an ambulance, headed to the Heart Hospital of Swedish American in Rockford, Illinois.

CHAPTER

TWENTY-FIVE

As the ambulance left my doctor's office in Byron and traveled to the hospital, the EMTs went about their work. They inserted an IV and began a drip. They hooked up an EKG machine and started the readout. I was given a nitroglycerin tablet which immediately alleviated the pain. When we arrived, I was whisked into the emergency room, and numerous technicians and nurses began their work. I was having--and had apparently been having-- a minor heart attack. After several tests (I don't honestly know exactly what they were) I was admitted and taken to a room. It was determined that I would have an angiogram to better understand exactly the issues.

Because my cardiologist had a full schedule, and since it was Friday, the angiogram was to take place on Monday. I spent the weekend in the hospital feeling great. Monday morning, I was taken to the cath lab for the angiogram. I expected to have a stent or two put in. Much to my surprise, the results showed I had four blockages which would necessitate open heart surgery with a quadruple bypass. The four blockages were 95%,

90%-the LAD (widow-maker again), 80%, and 90%. Serious business. Not at all average!

Because I was already on a couple of blood thinners, surgery had to wait until those medications were out of my system. That meant staying in the hospital for nearly a week. The surgery was scheduled for June 16, 2016. I'd be lying if I didn't admit I was somewhat anxious about the unknown. I had a team of doctors who explained the procedure. There was a cardio-thoracic surgeon, a couple more cardiologists, a nephrologist (kidney doctor), an anesthesiologist, and a squadron of nurses and medical technicians.

CHAPTER

TWENTY-SIX

Let me try to explain what coronary artery bypass graft surgery (CABG) is. It's a procedure used to treat coronary heart disease—the narrowing of coronary arteries. CABG x 4 is what the docs and nurses call it. It means a quadruple bypass, which is what I had. An intravenous line (IV) is inserted into your arm. Other catheters will be put in your neck and wrist to monitor your heart and blood pressure, as well as take blood samples. The anesthesiologist continuously monitors your heart rate, blood pressure, breathing, and blood oxygen level during your surgery. Once you are sedated, a breathing tube will be put into your throat and you will be connected to a ventilator, which will breathe for you during the surgery. A catheter will be put into your bladder to drain urine. Once all the tubes and monitors are in place, the doctor will make incisions in one or both of your legs (both in my case) to access the blood vessels to be used for the grafts. After removing the vessels, the doctor closes those incisions. Having those incisions heal is one of the most uncomfortable issues in the healing process. Next, an incision is made down the center of your chest from just below the Adam's apple to just above the navel. The doctor will cut the sternum (breastbone) in half lengthwise. The halves of the sternum will be spread apart to expose your heart.

In order to sew the grafts onto the very small coronary arteries, your heart must temporarily be stopped. Tubes will be inserted into the heart so that your blood can be pumped through your body by a heart-lung bypass machine. A tube is inserted into the aorta to carry the oxygenated blood from the aorta for circulation to the body. The heart-lung machine allows the heart's beating to be stopped, so the surgeon can operate on a still heart. Clamps are used to restrict blood flow to the area of the heart where the grafts will be placed so the heart is blood-free during the surgery. Once the blood has been diverted into the bypass machine for pumping, the doctor will stop your heart by injecting it with a cold solution. When the heart has been stopped, the doctor will do the bypass graft procedure by sewing one end of a section of vein over a tiny opening made in the aorta, and the other end over a tiny opening made in the coronary artery just below the blockage. After the four grafts have been completed, the doctor will closely check them as blood runs through them to make sure they're working. Once the grafts are all checked, the blood circulating through the bypass machine is allowed back into your heart, and the tubes to the machine are removed. Your heart may restart on its own, or a mild electrical shock may to necessary to restart it.

Your breastbone is then sewn together with small wires. Tubes are inserted into your chest to drain blood and other fluids from around the heart. The skin over the sternum in then sewn back together, and the doctor then puts a tube through your mouth into your stomach to drain stomach fluids. A temporary pacemaker is attached to the pacing wires to regulate the heart rhythm until the patient's condition improves. A sterile bandage or dressing is applied to the entire chest area.

After spending time in a recovery room, the patient recovers in a surgical intensive care unit (ICU) or CCU as it's called at Swedish American's Heart Hospital for several days. You will be connected to chest and breathing tubes, a mechanical ventilator (breathing machine), a heart monitor, and an electrocardiogram (EKG) machine. Other machines will monitor your blood pressure, oxygen level, and breathing rate. The urinary catheter remains in place. Drugs are prescribed to control pain and to prevent unwanted blood clotting. Bypass surgery is increasingly common. I was told nearly 500,000 bypass surgeries take place yearly.

However, can you imagine the reaction to the first person who had bypass surgery? The doctor tells them we just invented a new machine which allows us to shut down your heart, so we can operate on it. We're confident the machine will do all the things your heart normally does. We'll cut you open, saw your breastbone open, pry your ribs apart and put some veins on the arteries to bypass the blockages. Don't worry, we're pretty sure this will work!

Obviously, I was knocked out for the actual surgery. My most vivid memories are of the cold, narrow operating table. Half my butt hung over. And it was very cold. I had been given some "happy medicine" earlier to relax me and soon after arriving, I was put to sleep for the procedure. End of memory.

TWENTY-SEVEN

That's exactly what happened to me. The surgery took about seven hours. My son and daughter who live in the St. Louis area and my son who lives in the Chicago area were all at the hospital. My wife was, of course, there. I remember speaking with all of them before being wheeled off to the operating room. When I came to, they were all there. The doctors had spoken with them and said the surgery was a success. I was obviously elated to hear that. Due to the pain meds, I wasn't very coherent, but I recall that statement vividly. I had a breathing tube which presses upon the vocal chords, making it impossible to utter a sound. I was told patients frequently have the urge to remove the tube, so both my hands and feet were shackled to the bed to prevent an attempt to grab it. I never actually had the urge to do that. The tube reduced my communication to nodding my head yes or no. I was hooked up to God knows how many different monitors and machines--didn't know then, and don't know now, exactly what they did.

The time in recovery went by slowly, but I felt no pain because of the medications. Several hours after the surgery, I was asked to attempt to stand so I could be weighed on the large movable scale. I was unshackled and disconnected in order to stand. Try as I might, I couldn't get upright. Finally, with assistance from a couple of the staff, I was mostly standing. When asked to step on the scale, I simply could not get my foot up the required three or four inches and fell back into bed. From that simple exertion, I was exhausted.

Immediately, there was a large confab of doctors, nurses, techs, and who knows else. After a short time, I was told that the grafts were throwing clots, and they needed to check them out to figure out why. Perhaps one or more of the grafts hadn't been sewn tightly enough, I was told. The doctor explained that this was a possible life-threatening situation. Surgery would be planned for the next day. Probably because I was semi-numbed by pain medications, I accepted this worrisome information matter-of-factly. I realized what I was told was incredibly serious, but I still had the attitude that, "Hey, I've got this. Just another bump in the road".

CHAPTER

TWENTY-EIGHT

Early the next morning, I was again prepped for surgery. My wife and children were again present, and I remember my son Jeff kept saying, "You're a tough old bastard; you can do this." I didn't know at the time that the doctor had told them bluntly that this was very serious and that there was no guarantee I'd make it. I was essentially having open-heart quadruple by-pass surgery again within twenty-four hours. Believe me, that's exhausting—and not average.

I was sedated, and they re-opened my chest and examined all the grafts. The grafts were all sound. They deduced the reason for all the clots was my lupus. For no known reason, my body was attacking itself—the classic lupus behavior. I was wired and sewn back together, and they prescribed prednisone to control the lupus. After the seven-hour surgery, I was again returned to the ICU (known as the CCU--Critical Care Unit--at Swedish American Heart Hospital). As one can imagine, I was heavily sedated with pain medications. I would float into and out of consciousness. The breathing tube and restraints were back in place, I do remember that. I "woke up" from time to time during the next few days. I recall immediately being asked if I wanted more pain meds, and I'd nod my head yes. Then it was back to sleep again. During my stay in the CCU, a nurse was literally in my room all day. Actually, there were two of them assigned, and they each worked a twelve-hour shift. That's in addition to the normal floor nurses who were constantly in and out. The Swedish American hospital is a part of the U-W Madison hospital system, so there was also a monitor and camera in my room allowing specialists in Madison to watch and communicate with my nurses and doctors. It was the best care imaginable.

While I was not technically in a medically induced coma, I was by and large comatose for a couple of days. Whenever I woke up (regained consciousness), I was promptly given more meds and quickly went back to La-La Land. During the times I was "asleep," I had many bizarre dreams and conversations with myself. I remember having conversations with God. I'm not much for praying as such, although for years I have had "conversations" with God, thanking Him, or in some cases, asking for His assistance. These conversations usually occur when I'm alone. In this situation, I recall talking with Him about whether I was going to make it or not. It was very surreal, and I struggle now to attempt to explain exactly what went on in my mind. I genuinely remember talking with God. It's been over two years since then as I write this, and I don't recall the situation clearly, but it was very real and profound at the time. Perhaps all the pain medications helped to facilitate my conversations in this rather bizarre encounter.

One of the things my wife and I had talked about for years, but hadn't acted on, was our will, so a lawyer friend was gracious enough to come to the hospital the day before my first surgery, and we formally had a will and power-of-attorney drawn up. It was a relief. After I regained a sense of normalcy several days after the second surgery, Fran and I had a long conversation about my wishes for a funeral and services.

Our discussion about my final wishes got me to thinking about my hometown of Keokuk, Iowa, which is located in the southeast tip of Iowa at the confluence of the Mississippi and Des Moines rivers. There are two bridges: cross the Mississippi to the East, and one is in Illinois. Cross the Des Moines to the South, and one is in Missouri. In 1883 Keokuk was named in honor of the Sac Chief Keokuk. He was an exception to most of the chiefs because he looked for justice through wisdom and friendship with the white man. Keokuk is about an hour's drive from Hannibal, Missouri, so there's a lot of Mark Twain history involved. The first City Directory was published by Orion Clemens with help from his brother Sam, better known as Mark Twain. Twain actually lived in Keokuk for nearly two years and in 1889 bought a house for his mother which still exists today as a private residence. The grandfather of the famous Howard Hughes lived in Keokuk and served as mayor and was president of the Keokuk & Western Railroad. The family burial plot is in Keokuk's Oakland Cemetery.

One of the largest tourist attractions, literally, is Lock and Dam No.19 on the Mississippi River. It's an immense structure covering over 1,500 acres. Construction began in 1910 and was completed three years later. The workable portion of the dam is 4,620 feet long and has 119 movable gates to control water flow. When completed it was second in length in the entire world and was the largest capacity single powerhouse electricity generating plant in the world.

Keokuk, Iowa was--and is--a rough, tough, nasty, Mississippi River town. I say that with pride and admiration. It most certainly influenced the way I am today. Having grown up there, I know it's part of why I'm not average. I learned to swim in the muddy Mississippi and how to water ski. My friends and I virtually lived on the river in summers--boating, fishing, living a great life. If you've ever been on that river and been able to zoom over miles and miles of water without impediment, if you've ever gone through the vast lock system in a pleasure boat, if you've ever been up close to the overpowering immensity of that dam, then you know that there is absolutely nothing average about the Mississippi River.

The other main tourist attraction is the Keokuk National Cemetery. It's been there since the Civil War. In fact, it's one of the original twelve established in 1862 by Abraham Lincoln

In the Civil War, Keokuk was an important destination due to its location on the Mississippi River. Over 80,000 Union soldiers shipped out from Keokuk to various destinations. Thousands of casualties were also delivered by riverboat back to Keokuk, which had seven hospitals and two colleges of medicine during the Civil war. As soldiers died, they had to be buried. Eventually, 627 Union soldiers were buried, 27 of whom were unknown. Eight Confederate prisoners-of-war were also interred. Today, approximately 100 burials are conducted annually.

Keokuk's cemetery is a smaller version of Arlington with gentle rolling hills, well-manicured, and with row upon row of white marble headstones. I've always found it to be peaceful, and in a sense, spiritual. The Keokuk National Cemetery now has well over 4,000 military veterans and spouses buried there including a Medal of Honor winner from WWII and one of Teddy Roosevelt's "Rough Riders." It has a Monument to the Unknowns, also. My father is buried there, my mother is buried there, and I also plan to be buried there. For veterans, the plot, headstone, and vault are provided by the VA at no charge.

This military cemetery and military burial were on my mind after my quadruple bypass surgery. After two days, once my surgical recovery progressed enough that the breathing tube was removed, and I could talk, Fran and I spoke of my funeral wishes: my desire to be buried at the Keokuk National Cemetery, to have a military funeral, who I would prefer to be the pall bearers, and several other elements of the service. It was a good feeling to share these ideas and concepts with her.

TWENTY-NINE

After I had the breathing tube and shackles removed, Fran and I had discussed my final wishes, and I felt ironically as if I had been born again. For one thing, I could talk. That's when Fran and I had our conversations about my funeral and about my wishes for not living as a vegetable, hooked to machines breathing for me. On about the 21st of June, some five days after my surgeries, I had a serious conversation with one of the doctors on my "team." It was the kidney specialist, and he was blunt and direct, which I appreciated. "Charley," he said, "your kidneys have shut down. Right now, we can save your kidneys, but you will die. Or we can save you now and worry about the kidneys later." Wow! What a choice. Obviously, we went for the "save me now" option. I had a minor surgical procedure to implant what is called a portal in order to be able to undergo dialysis. The portal allows blood to be removed and returned quickly, efficiently, and safely during dialysis. The dialysis machine circulates one's blood through the machine to remove impurities and regulate chemical and fluid balances. The purified blood is then returned to the patient through the dialysis access.

I had daily dialysis for three days. Thankfully my kidneys responded more positively every day, and on the fourth day the doctors decided to stop dialysis and see what would happen. Amazingly, my kidneys responded well, and it was determined that I probably wouldn't need dialysis anymore. It's a life-saving procedure, but really time consuming and boring.

On the 23rd of June, several nurses and techs came to my room and helped me to stand. It was a major accomplishment, but I was unable to do it without their help. With a walker and their assistance, I was able to slowly walk about twenty feet before returning to bed exhausted. It was so bizarre—I couldn't "just walk." Somehow my brain and muscles didn't seem to be on the same page. It was like learning to walk all over again. I was compelled to concentrate on each stumbling, shuffling step. I was like a toddler again. It was incredibly frustrating. My body—my legs specifically—simply wouldn't respond as they had for over seventy years before the surgeries and complications. As adults we don't normally think about the act of walking. We just walk. At that time, I couldn't walk without concentrating intently on each and every step. Concentrating on foot placement. Thinking about keeping my balance. It was mentally and physically exhausting.

THIRTY

The next day, June 24th, the pace-maker from the open-heart surgery was removed. The chest drains were also removed. During this entire ordeal I had experienced virtually no pain. Obviously, I had been under general anesthetic for the open-heart surgery. Later I had been given lots of pain medicines which greatly helped. That "no pain" situation came to a crashing halt on June 24th. My entire chest area from collarbone to navel was covered in some type of white surgical tape. That was removed. How? One of the male nurses began pulling it off. Pain? Oh, my, yes. It was excruciating. When finally completed, I had several spots on my chest and stomach that were oozing blood from literally having the skin ripped off.

Later that day, I again spent time with my walker and was able to go slightly farther then the first day. The actual walking still required all my concentration. I went for short walks twice that day, with a much-needed nap in between my small journeys.

On the following day, one of the best events of my ordeal occurred. The nurses gave my wife, Fran, permission to give me a sponge bath. It was glorious. It had been over a week since I'd bathed (or been bathed), and it was well needed. The staff had me up on my walker for my journey three times daily. Each time I went a little farther (maybe only six or eight feet), and it was very gradually getting easier. Walking still required my concentration, unlike what we normally do. Imagine if one had to concentrate on breathing. Consciously sucking in the air and then intentionally expelling it. That's how I was trying to walk. Each small step was planned and executed individually. There was no natural "flow." The kidney doctor also had good news that my kidney function was continuing to improve and that there would be no dialysis again the next day. Very good news.

I didn't spend much time thinking about all the frustrating things I was experiencing. My competitive nature took over. I concentrated on going a little farther each walk. I tried to go a bit faster and more naturally each time. If the physical therapist asked me to try and walk around the nurses' station once, I damn sure tried to do it more than once. I was not going to simply do what an average patient would do. I'm not average; "I got this," my subconscious self would scream at me.

On June 26—ten days after my surgeries—I walked four times. Each time was a little farther than before, even if only a few steps. I was intent on beating my previous mark—setting a new PR (personal record), as we say in track.

My walking skills were slowly improving, but it still required my full concentration not to stumble or trip with every step I took. It was so frustrating. As adults who have walked without thinking about the natural process for nearly all our lives, it's hard to fathom the experience of having to think about each and every step one takes.

More good news from the kidney doc that day: my kidneys continued to respond and were improving. No dialysis planned for the next day. Such a relief. The dialysis process takes between three and four hours. That's a long time lying still and doing nothing. It seemed even longer when I was having dialysis.

CHAPTER

THIRTY-ONE

An ongoing problem during all of this was the fact that a few months earlier, I had become an insulin-dependent diabetic. The endocrinologist (diabetes doctor) was in the process of attempting to stabilize my blood sugar with my daily insulin injections. However, once it was determined that my lupus had kicked in causing the blood clot issues, the solution for the problem was prednisone. Yet, prednisone totally messes up one's blood sugar/insulin routine. As a result, I was registering blood sugar readings in the 300s and a few in the 400 range. Not average, and also, not good. Consequently, I was being checked several times daily for my blood sugar numbers and then being injected with insulin to attempt to get the readings back into a satisfactory range.

On the 27th of July, my dialysis portal was removed. I found it a painful procedure, but it was worth it because it signaled that dialysis was indeed a thing of the past. I continued my daily walks, still with the aid of a walker. As before, I tried each walk to go a little farther than previously. I was now making as least three and usually four journeys through the halls of the hospital.

The next day was a milestone. With the aid of two gracious women from the physical therapy department, I had a real, honest-to-goodness shower. They took me by wheelchair to a shower, and I was warned beforehand that it would be surprisingly tiring. It was. I was told to sit on a stool for the process. They explained that the warm water and humidity would be very debilitating, and they were right. In fact, I still use a stool to sit on as I shower to this day—over two years after my surgeries as I write this. The shower felt wonderful. I even had an actual shampoo and a shave. When I was returned to my room, I promptly fell asleep for a three- hour nap. Later the chief doctor from the rehab hospital dropped by to give me an examination and ask lots of questions about my progress to that time. It was being discussed that I would be released from Swedish American Hospital and transferred to Van Matre rehabilitation hospital for an undetermined period of time.

On June 29, I learned that my kidney function was continuing to improve, and dialysis was absolutely not a concern. As my kidney function improved, my daily prednisone dosage was gradually being decreased. Thankfully, that allowed my blood sugar readings to also improve and become closer to the normal range. I had three long (for me) walks that day, and I continued to improve my walking "skills." It still required my utmost concentration not to trip or stumble, but all-in-all I was getting better, and my walking was gradually getting more "normal." The other big deal of the day was learning I had been accepted at the rehab hospital.

I had been told by people with first-hand knowledge how hard one was worked at the rehab facility. I was told to expect at least three, perhaps four, workouts daily. I was looking forward to the challenge but was also a bit nervous. In my mind, I was remembering the days of twice--daily basketball practices in college and Army basic training. Would this upcoming regimen be like that? If it was, could my seventy-year old body handle it? I didn't sleep very well that night.

June 30 of 2016 was my last day at Swedish American Heart Hospital. I had another great shower and did my three walking trips. Walking continued to get easier, but it was still very tiring both physical and mentally. I was still concerned about how difficult the actual physical therapy program would be. On the plus side, I'd been told by several people that the food at the rehab hospital was superb--fine restaurant quality. Starting the next day, I guessed that I'd be able to judge for myself.

CHAPTER
THIRTY-TWO

I had arrived at the Rehabilitation Hospital. I was delivered via wheelchair in a specially equipped van. Not sure if it was cool or embarrassing. I arrived in early afternoon and after getting a room assignment, had the rest of the day to myself. Couldn't help but keep wondering how intense and difficult the workouts would be. I was getting myself "psyched up" for whatever they had to challenge me. The food was every bit as delicious as advertised, especially the desserts. Also, I was now on a daily regimen of 80 milligrams of Lasix twice a day. Lasix is a powerful diuretic which made me urinate about every 45 minutes or so, 24 hours a day. I was retaining fluid, especially in my lower body and legs, and the Lasix was a method to remove the fluid. Boy, did it work. It is difficult to get a good, restful night's sleep, when one is compelled to get up and go to the bathroom every forty-five minutes or so. Such was now to be my daily routine.

July 2, 2016 was my first legitimate day of rehab. There was both physical rehab and occupational rehab. Physical rehab included walking in the gym, going up and down stairs, getting in and out of bed, walking up and down an incline, walking on smooth surfaces and transitioning to carpet; occupational rehab consisted of working with fine motor skills--using small nuts and bolts to practice using the fingers with small objects, matching decks of cards into suites and rows of correct numbers, practicing using normal kitchen gadgets and household things like fingernail clippers. It quickly became obvious that my left hand was very deficient in both strength and dexterity.

I normally had two daily sessions of both physical and occupational therapy. Both types were conducted in the gym area. Part of the gym looked like a gym with typical gym equipment. Another whole section was a small home with kitchen counters, cabinets, stove, fridge, and other normal household objects. I walked several laps in the gym, using my walker, which was getting easier every trip. I also practiced getting into and out of bed. That was surprisingly difficult. The four sessions were somewhat spread out through the day, so I had some opportunity to rest between workouts. My fears that this would be akin to Army basic training were put to rest. However, the sessions were certainly intense, difficult, and tiring.

Surprisingly, on July 3, I had no therapy of any kind. It was a completely restful and relaxing day. Fran was there as she had been every day since my ordeal had begun several weeks ago. I was able to shave for the first time in a week, which was refreshing. I did walk through the halls twice on my own because it seemed the thing to do. I was intent on doing my best to rehab and get home, so I didn't want to spend an entire day doing nothing. In my mind, that's what most average patients would have done, and I'm not average.

Happy 4th of July! Turned out the holiday was yesterday on the 3rd. I had four therapy sessions on the 4th. Very demanding. Walking continued to improve, but still needed a walker. Wouldn't even consider attempting to walk without a walker. My balance was still not very good. In addition to the usual physical activities like walking, doing the stairs, and getting in and out of bed, my therapist added a new wrinkle today. I was put on a recumbent bike for ten minutes. It was actually almost enjoyable. I was given a predetermined speed, and I was able to keep my speed at that rate.

Perhaps because I was working harder, my appetite was increasing. In any case, I always looked forward to meal time after my therapy sessions.

It seemed like every day the therapists added some new torture to my routine. July 5th was no exception. In addition to the walking and stairs, I did the recumbent bike. The time was again ten minutes, but the resistance was increased making it more difficult to pedal and more tiring overall.

The newest torture involved my legs, and the exercises I was assigned were killers. I was seated on a chair and instructed to squeeze my legs together to hold--and then lift--a large ball that had been placed on the floor between my legs. Might sound easy, but it wasn't for this ol' guy. I did several "sets" of three or four "repetitions" each, and the muscles in my thighs were on fire. As if that weren't enough, they then placed a large rubber band around both legs at the knees and instructed me to spread my knees and hold them apart. Once again, it may sound easy, but it wasn't for me. I'm a guy who at the age of fifty-seven was able to squat 450 pounds in the weight room. Now I could barely spread my knees with a stupid rubber band around them. A 450-pound squat is not average, especially for a fifty-seven-year-old man, but neither was barely being able to open one's knees with a rubber band around them. I knew I still had a lot of work to do before I would be able to go home. On a more positive note, I was able to take a real shower (while sitting on a stool) and shampoo. It almost made the gym workout worthwhile.

Another day, another series of four sessions. On July 6, I had three physical workouts and one occupational session. The physical therapy sessions were mostly like all the others, but one new element was added. I was put on a device called a Nustep which is basically a recumbent stepper or climber. It had a mechanism to keep track of the time and also one to control the tension which allowed the amount of pressure required to move the pedals to be adjusted. I found it challenging to attempt to beat the preset time and speed. It was demanding, but I liked it. On this machine it would be easy to determine one's progress, either in time, speed, or tension in each subsequent workout. I actually looked forward to my next workout on the Nustep.

I'd been at the rehab hospital for a week, and on July 7th I was scheduled for three workouts-- two physical and one occupational. Walking continued

CHAPTER

THIRTY-THREE

On July 9th, 2016, I was released from the rehab hospital and sent home. It was a great feeling to be at home. However, there were a couple of issues to manage. The first was the layout of our house. It was a two-story, and the bedroom and master bathroom were both upstairs. Luckily there was a half bath on the ground floor. Fran had purchased a beautiful new oversized recliner that reclined simply by pushing a button. That chair would allow me to sleep on the main floor until I was both physically and mentally prepared to attack the thirteen steps leading up to the master bedroom and bathroom.

Another issue was my medications. I was taking eighteen different medications each day—some of them twice daily. In addition to taking multiple pills, I had to check my blood sugar three times daily and give myself insulin injections five times daily. We worked out a place to store all the meds, and I secured a box in which to put each day's pills for a week at a time.

I spent some time with my walker that day, going from my house down the sidewalk to the neighbor's driveway and back. I'd rest on a chair in my garage, then make the trek again. I did this about eight times. I spent that first night at home sleeping in the recliner, and it was awesome.

The 10th, 11th, and 12th of July I spent resting and walking. As before, I used a chair in my garage to rest in-between sessions. My competitive juices began to flow, and I decided to try some old track practice concepts. The first day I walked the same course to the neighbor's driveway, but I also used a stop watch to check my time each trip and to determine how long I rested between sessions. My goal was to walk a little faster each trip. I made about eight trips, and I was able to set a new personal record each time. By the end of the day, I was very tired but felt rewarded with my above-average performance.

On July 11 I changed my workout procedure. Instead of going the same route and trying to go a little faster than I had the day before, I changed my route. My goal now was to go farther each trip—to go past my next-door neighbor's driveway to the next one, and then the next one, and so on. I did record my time for each trip on my stop watch, but speed wasn't my goal; distance was. Once again, I was successful. As the day before, I made about eight trips, and I was able to go a little farther each trip. I was again very tired at the end of the day but upbeat because I was able to see my progress.

After a good night's sleep, the next day (July 12), I changed my "workout routine" once more. I attempted to go for both distance and time. I had timed myself the day before as I went to my various neighbors' driveways. That day I was determined to go a little faster as I made the same trips as the day before. The results were somewhat mixed. The first few trips I was able to beat my time from the day before. As fatigue set in, I began to be unable to improve my time from the day before. I even "fudged" my recovery time in the chair in my garage as I rested between trips a couple of times, thinking a couple of extra minutes of rest would allow me to beat my previous time. Unfortunately, it didn't work. I was exhausted at day's end and somewhat disappointed, but all in all it was a successful performance. I was definitely getting stronger and better at the simple act of walking—even if I was still using a walker.

One of the reasons I was working so hard on my walking was to improve and be more independent. Why? In late July, a class reunion was scheduled for the very first senior class I had taught in Cherokee, Iowa. My "kids," the class of 1968, had invited me to attend, and I was determined to go. My wife had used so many of her sick and vacation days because of my hospitalization that I would be going by myself. So, I needed to be able to function on my own. As a sign of how long I'd been teaching, these "kids" were now on Medicare. I'd only been four years older than they when I taught in the 1967-68 school year. I was honored and excited to make the trip. But I needed to be able to be pretty damn independent.

On the 13 of July I had a scheduled appointment with my cardiologist. I had an echocardiogram, an EKG, several x-rays, and all was good. I went for a couple of walks after returning from the doctor and felt great. At bed time I slowly made my way up the thirteen steps to the second floor to finally spend a night in my own bed, rather than sleep on the recliner. The diuretic (Lasix) dosage had been lowered, and as a result I was able to sleep about two hours without having to go to the bathroom. All in all, another great day.

On July 15th, the day didn't start well. I felt listless and had no energy. I didn't know what was wrong, but I didn't feel right. I was scheduled for an appointment with my diabetes doctor, and they did the usual vitals: heart rate, oxygen level, blood pressure. My blood pressure was 80/40. Not good. I was immediately sent to the emergency room where an IV was inserted. An hour later my blood pressure reading was in the normal range, and I was sent home. The doctors weren't too sure, but they thought the low blood pressure was due to the diuretics.

The next day, July 16th, was a busy one. The Visiting Nurses Association home care nurse came to the house. She brought a machine that every day would take my blood pressure, heart rate, oxygen level, and weight to electronically send them to my doctor's office. I would have to be hooked up every day between 10:00 and 10:30 AM to register these vitals. No more sleeping in. I realized it was a necessary evil, but I didn't like the whole daily monitor program. It was just another daily pain-in-the butt like the five insulin shots and three blood sugar checks. Seemed like all I did was poke myself and/or hook up to medical devices.

CHAPTER

THIRTY-FOUR

On July 21 I left Rockford to begin my odyssey to Cherokee. I hadn't been allowed to drive until thirty days after my surgery. So, on July 17th, I had driven myself to run some errands and had been driving about town every day since. I had decided to break up the trip by driving about three hours to Des Moines and spending the night with one of my old college roommates, Tom Ahlers. After graduating in 1967, Tom had moved to Des Moines. He began refereeing high school football games and moved up the ladder and eventually refereed college football in the Big 8 (now the Big 12). He went all the way to the top and was the referee in three national championship games. His day job was as a CPA where he was the managing partner for a large firm. Several years ago, he had retired from football refereeing and was also semi-retired from his CPA work. It was great to see him. I planned to get up the next day and finish the several hour drive to Cherokee. It was great seeing my old friend whom I hadn't seen in some time. We went out to dine and spent a lot of time catching up.

Once in Cherokee, one of my former students and her husband had graciously offered to have me spend my visit at their home. The weekend there was a blast. I saw many former students and another of my colleagues with whom I had taught and coached at Cherokee. I was honored and surprised at how many from the class of 1968 had gone into education and said I was part of the inspiration for their career choice. Pretty cool, and it gave me a very positive and uplifted feeling. I even went so far as to walk (very carefully) without using my walker while in Cherokee.

The drive to Des Moines and then to Cherokee had been pleasant and enjoyable. It was nice to be on my own and feel independent and able to do things on my own again. I've always liked being on the road by myself, but this trip was more enjoyable than usual. It was interstate and/or divided highways all the way, so it was easy driving and offered hours of time for introspection.

My return trip was another two-parter. I drove from Cherokee to Dubuque where I spent the night with another former college roommate and basketball teammate, Dr. Laddie Sula. After graduating from Loras, Laddie had gone to the University of Illinois and earned his master's degree. He then received his Ph.D. from Georgia State University in Atlanta. He taught economics for a few years at Boise State and then returned to teach at Loras where he remained for over 30 years. He had retired a couple of years ago. It was always good to see old friends and catch up. The next day it was an easy drive back home to Rockford, Illinois. I felt great after my long weekend trip. Psychologically, it was a positive experience to be totally on my own for several days. It was an empowering experience to be independent again, even if only for a few days.

THIRTY-FIVE

About the 15th of August, I received a check from the VA for nearly $25,000. A couple of days later I received a document from the VA explaining what was happening. After several months of encouragement from my brother-in-law, who was also a Vietnam vet, I had finally filed a claim for disability because of my unexplained diabetes and heart condition. There was no history of either in my family background. Curt, my brother-in-law, had stipulated that the diabetes claim was nearly a "rubber stamp" because of Agent Orange exposure for nearly anyone who had served in Vietnam. I had filed in 2015 and had been told it might take months, up to a year, to find out the VA's decision. If one received a "rating" of a certain percentage of disability, one received "back pay" for the disability from the date of the claim. That's exactly what had happened to me. The check was for the back pay of my disability claim. The VA had given me a disability rating of 70% for the combined issues of diabetes and heart conditions because of my exposure to Agent Orange during my tour of duty in Vietnam. I would also be receiving a monthly check beginning on the 1st of September. It was a nice monetary award, but I'd have given it up in a New York minute to be without diabetes and all my heart issues. The VA's deliberation was actually made *before* my open--heart surgery and subsequent difficulties, so I was optimistic that my rating of 70% might be raised if I appealed—which I planned to do. Why appeal? Simple—more money each month.

CHAPTER

THIRTY-SIX

On August 15, I began teaching again at South Beloit High School. That was the 2016-17 school year. I was to teach three classes, two sophomore English and one honors sophomore English. It was the same load I'd had for several years. School began at 8:00, and I was finished at 11:02. That gave me the rest of the day to work at my other job as a real estate broker. All was good.

I started cardiopulmonary rehab on August 31. It went well. My blood sugar was tested along with my blood pressure, heart rate, and oxygen level before each session began. About half-way through the session, blood pressure was taken again, and then yet again at the end of the workout. I began with my old friend the Nustep for five minutes. Next was the treadmill for five minutes, then a machine that had me crank a device that worked the arms and shoulders. I went three times a week, and every day the time, the speed, or the resistance was increased. I finished cardiac rehab before school started, so, when I returned to teaching, I was feeling super.

As an example of how well rehab was going, one day on the treadmill the nurse asked me how much longer I had to go. I looked at the timer on the machine and told her 40 seconds. She looked and said, "40 seconds until 15 minutes! You were scheduled to do 5 minutes."

The next time I was at rehab, two days later, I was tired and listless at the beginning. My legs were heavy, and I had no energy. After three minutes on the treadmill, I had to stop. I simply couldn't go on. The therapists were understanding, and I reluctantly left to go home.

On October 15th, Fran's daughter, Sierra, was married. All my children and their children were there. It was a wonderful time. It was the first time all our children, both mine and hers, and all 12 grandchildren were together. Lots of pictures were taken. I was mentally excited, but physically, I felt horrible. My ankles and legs were swollen, I'd gained weight, I had almost no energy. I left the reception early because I was so tired.

Three days after the wedding, I had a scheduled appointment with my cardiologist. I still felt lousy, and they did lots of tests. At the end I was told that I was suffering from AFib—arterial fibrillation. Like most people, I'd heard of AFib, but didn't really know exactly it was. They explained that it's an irregular and often rapid heart rate that can increase the risk of stroke, heart failure, and other heart-rated complications. Symptoms include weakness, reduced ability to exercise, fatigue, and shortness of breath--and I had all of those. AFib itself isn't usually life-threatening, but it is a serious medical condition. It can lead to blood clots forming in the heart that may circulate to other organs and lead to strokes. Some of the causes of AFib can be high blood pressure, heart disease, diabetes, kidney disease, and age, among others. Of course, I had all of these.

My doctors determined that I was a candidate for a procedure called a cardioversion, or more specifically, an electrical cardioversion. It's a corrective procedure where an electrical shock is delivered to the heart to change an abnormal heart rhythm back to normal. Mine was scheduled for October 24th. I arrived at the hospital in the morning. I hadn't eaten or drunk anything since midnight. The procedure was an outpatient one, meaning I would not be overnight in the hospital. I was given a saline solution IV at the beginning. I was then given some nasty stuff to gargle which helped to numb my throat. Next, they placed a device to hold open my mouth, and then they sprayed more deadening stuff into my mouth aiming at the back. A metal patch about 4x6 inches was secured on my chest, and another one like it was affixed to my back. A few minutes later they explained that soon I would be getting very sleepy and while "asleep" they would feed a long tube into my throat which would enable them to see if there were blood clots which could potentially break loose. Assuming there were none, an electrical shock would be administered in the hope that the shock would jolt my heart back into a reg

They found no problem with blood clots, and the procedure went ahead. Sometime later, when I came out of my "sleep", the doctors said the cardioversion was a success and that my heart rhythm was back to normal. I was happy, but mostly I was sleepy. I was released from the hospital, and I went home to a nice four-hour nap.

The next day, I felt great. Everything was back to more or less normal. The shortness of breath was gone, as was the listlessness and general feeling of blah. Sadly, this lasted about ten days and then I was back to the previous AFib symptoms, which have now been haunting me for over two years.

About a month later, in November, I was again gaining weight, my legs and ankles were extremely swollen, and I was feeling listless. I had an appointment with my doctor, and they administered numerous tests. I remember an EKG, an echocardiogram, and several X-rays. About 8:00 that night I received a call at home from my cardiologist. I was surprised that he himself called me. He said I should go to the emergency room right away. Since it was Thanksgiving week, I was reluctant and told him I really didn't want to go. He bluntly said, "Charley, if you don't go to the ER, in my estimation there's about a 15-20% chance you're going to die. Your lungs are so full of fluid, you're at risk of drowning." "I'll be there in 15 minutes," I answered. I arrived at the emergency room and was admitted. They hooked me to an IV and began to administer Lasix, the powerful diuretic with which I was so familiar. I had fluid in my chest and throughout my body. In the space of four days, I lost well over 20 pounds of fluid, primarily because of urinating about every 45 minutes day and night. I was released around 5:00 in the evening on Thanksgiving night.

Fran and I went to Cracker Barrel and had a late Thanksgiving dinner. I felt great.

The next three months were pretty cool. I was teaching every day and feeling good. But then the AFib symptoms kicked in again. I felt terrible. It was the worst yet. No energy at all. I had to rest in the school's office after walking into the building before continuing to my room. I couldn't stand up to teach, having to sit all period. I was miserable. My principal was understanding, so I took nearly four weeks off, hoping to feel better and get back to work rested and ready to go. Sadly, it didn't work. I continued to feel terrible. I had gone to the doctor in early March, and they ran numerous tests. I had an EKG, an echocardiogram, and several X-rays. Once again, the AFib was kicking my butt. I was again admitted to the hospital. They hooked up the IV with Lasix again, and in four days I lost 20+ pounds. I felt great again and was back to teaching once more. I finished the year and handed in my letter of resignation. I had always planned to teach for 50 years...just because. It seemed like a reasonable goal, a nice even number. I made it for 46 years of teaching, including the last ten years of part-time. Since I felt so vulnerable because of the AFib, I decided to be an old retired guy. Also, we were planning to move from Rockford to Sterling, Illinois. Sterling is Fran's home town, all of her children and grandchildren live there, and she works out of the DCFS office there. I had actually lived in Sterling myself for sixteen years while I taught at Newman High School and when I had commuted daily to teach in Byron, Illinois. Our house in Rockford had been on the market and finally sold, and we had found what would become our new home in Sterling. We were scheduled to close on our house in Sterling on August 29, 2017 and sell our home in Rockford on August 30th.

CHAPTER

THIRTY-
SEVEN

On the 20th of August I awoke about 3:00 in the morning with my old friend heartburn. I took some Gaviscon liquid and expected it to work its magic. Sadly, it didn't happen. I went into the office at home and chewed a few Gaviscon tablets, feeling confident that treatment would do the job. Much to my dismay, no relief. I continued taking Gaviscon off and on for over two hours. At 5:00 AM, I woke Fran, and we went to the ER.

After a battery of tests at the ER, I was admitted to the hospital for still more tests. It was determined that I had fluid inside the pericardial sack. That was what was causing the heart burn/heart attack pain. I was again hooked up to the Lasix IV and continued through more tests. There was an EKG and a medical stress test among others. The doctors again performed an angiogram and determined that it appeared a clot was forming once again in one of the grafts. Because of the negative impact the dye they use has on my kidneys, the docs decided to wait for some time before going in to install some stents. The stent procedure was scheduled for September

5th. We were scheduled to move to Sterling on August 29, which may have also been a factor in the delay.

On the day of the surgery, all went well, and a single stent was put in place. Again, because of the dye, the doctors decided to postpone to a later date putting in the two additional stents they had determined were required. I was in the hospital for a couple of days and released. The next stent procedure was scheduled for September 25.

On the 25^{th,} I was admitted to the hospital, and the doctors placed two more stents, including a new one in one of the four grafts from my previous open-heart surgery. That was a bit of a surprise to the doctors and to me. Supposedly the life of a graft is years, but I needed a stent in about fourteen months. My cardiologist thinks that's due to my lupus. So now, I have a total of six stents and a quadruple bypass. Because they had to go back in within 24 hours of the original surgery in June of 2016, doctors say it's as if I'd had quadruple bypass twice. I'm definitely not average.

THIRTY-EIGHT

In October of 2016, I had been granted temporary 100% disabled status by the VA based on my heart condition. It was for the period of June 8, 2016 to September 30, 2016, based on the hospitalization and my heart condition and medical issues. On October 1, 2016, my status reverted to a 60% evaluation for my heart issues, and combined with the diabetes evaluation, my total disability percentage was 70%.

In June of 2017, I was summoned to the VA hospital in Madison, Wisconsin, for an examination regarding my percentage of disability status. I had appealed my 60% rating since my heart condition had continued to deteriorate. The big question was the diagnosis of "acute myocardial infarction" with congestive heart failure. "Acute" is the key word because it only results in a 60% rating. After my examination at the VA hospital in Madison, it was determined that I have CHRONIC congestive heart failure, which merits a 100% rating. According to the VA system, that is based on "three METs [a MET is a unit of measurement of heat production by the body, being the heat produced by a resting-sitting subject. It's short for 'metabolic equivalent'] or less resulting in dyspnea, fatigue, and dizziness. Additional symptoms include: continuous medication is required, evidence of cardio hypertrophy on echocardiogram, left ventricular dysfunction with an ejection fraction of 30 to 50 percent, more than one episode of acute congestive heart failure within the past year." The 100% disability rating was back dated to March 14, 2017.

Why did I want a 100% disability rating? Simple…money. The monthly stipend for a 100% rating was over double what the 70% rating was. With a "standard" 100% rating, one can still work if they so choose. If one is classified as "unemployable" at 100%, one can't work, even if one wishes to. Since I had resigned, I would be losing the income from my teaching assignment at South Beloit High School, so the additional income from the VA would help to "take up the slack." Additionally, I would be eligible for a benefit that waived my real estate taxes.

In late August, after we had moved to Sterling, I was contacted by Newman Central Catholic High School to see if I was interested in teaching part-time. I had previously taught and coached there from 1978 to 1987. I had served as head boys' basketball coach, sophomore football coach, and athletic director during that time. Newman is an excellent school, both in academics and athletics. Head football coach Mike Papoccia has won over 300 games, including five state championships and two 2nd place finishes and is in the Illinois High School Football Coaches Hall of Fame. Under Coach Rich Montgomery, a member of the Illinois Wrestling Coaches Hall of Fame, the Comets won a state championship and a third place. Newman has also won state titles in track and cross country. Additionally, they have state trophies in girls' basketball, boys' basketball, and girls' softball. I had great and fond memories of my earlier time at Newman. In the 1979-80 basketball season we were fortunate to qualify for the Illinois State Basketball Tournament, the first time that had happened in school history. This past season the 2017-18 team made it even further, qualifying for the Final Four and winning 3rd place.

In 2005, my oldest son, Jeff, and I were both inducted into the Newman Central Catholic High School Hall of Fame. He was a phenomenal high school football player who heard from nearly 100 colleges during the recruiting process. He made all the All-State teams and accepted a full scholarship to play football of the University of Notre Dame. In fact, the great, long-time Chicago *Sun Times* sports writer, Taylor Bell, included Jeff in an article of the "Greatest in the History of Illinois High School Football" as one of the greatest offensive linemen in Illinois high school history. That induction was one of the proudest moments I can recall. It was tangible validation of not being average...for both of us.

My daughter, Kelly, attended Newman as a freshman, but transferred to Sterling High School and graduated from there. At Newman, she had played volleyball and basketball, but her true love was drama, plays, and artistic endeavors. She matriculated at my alma mater, Loras College.

Our youngest son, Jason, attended Newman as a freshman, also. He was a standout in basketball and football, but we moved to Byron, Illinois, when I accepted a job teaching there, and he graduated from Byron High school. He was also an All-State football player and received a scholarship to Truman State University in Missouri where he was an all-conference player as a tight end.

With that as background, I was very interested in returning to Newman as a part-time teacher. At the time of the August job offer, I had been to Madison for my VA re-evaluation but had not yet received their decision. During my evaluation, the doctor had indicated she was thinking of rating me as "unemployable." Now that designation conveyed both good and bad news. The good news was that "unemployable" meant one jumped to a 100% rating automatically. The bad news was one cannot work even if they feel able to do so.

Since I had that eventual diagnosis hanging over my head, I felt compelled to turn down the Newman opportunity. The possibility existed that I might start teaching and in September or October or November discover that I had been rated as unemployable. That would mean I would have to stop teaching, leaving Newman in the lurch having to find a teacher.

THIRTY-NINE

Shortly after declining the position at Newman High School, I received a packet in the mail from the VA. I was surprised since I had anticipated it would be a much longer wait. My hands were shaking as I ripped open the envelope with its distinctive VA return address. Much to my great pleasure, I was awarded a 100% disability rating based on the condition of my heart. It was back dated to March, so there would be some "back pay" also. It was a strange sensation. I was happy that I had received the 100% rating because my monthly payment would now be over double what it had been. But it was depressing to realize that I was now considered 100% disabled. I felt so old and helpless.

The prior April I had had my annual checkup with my VA doctor at the clinic in Rockford. All went well until he asked me about a pimple-looking bump under my right eye. I told him that it had come and gone several times in the past year. "Well, that's skin cancer," he bluntly responded. "Everyone knows a wound that won't heal is skin cancer." I definitely didn't know. He indicated he'd tell the VA hospital in Madison, Wisconsin, and they would contact me to set up an appointment. I thought, "This isn't average for sure." The old saying "If it wasn't for bad luck, I wouldn't have any" crossed my mind.

In the usual bureaucratic way, it took months for the VA to reach me and set an appointment. My appointment was actually changed after it was scheduled, so I went to Madison in September for the procedure. It was an outpatient procedure and described to me as a simple one. They planned to numb my cheek area, make an incision, take a sample of the tissue, and conduct a biopsy. That's exactly what they did. After examining my body, they decided that a particular mole on my lower back also looked suspicious, so a sample was to be taken from there also. After the tissue was removed, I had about an hour's wait while the biopsy was performed. The results showed that there was definitely skin cancer in the spot on my cheek, and the mole on my back was worth removing due to "probable" cancer.

The good news was that the cancer was not melanoma, but basal, the "good" kind. I was left with a dime-sized wound under my right eye and a quarter-sized wound on my back.

I was to apply vaseline petroleum jelly daily and simply put a band-aid over the opening. In a matter of days, the incisions would be healed. Another appointment was made for the cancerous tissues themselves to be removed. On October 10, I returned to Madison for the procedure.

Once again this was to be an outpatient procedure. The affected area would be numbed with injections, and then a process called the Mohs surgery would be performed. It's named after the doctor who invented it, and they explained how it happens. The surgeon removes a bit of visible cancerous tissue which is sent to an on-site laboratory and a biopsy is performed. If cancer cells are detected, they doctor removes another layer of tissue, and another biopsy is performed. This continues until no cancerous tissue remains.

The surgeon removed tissue from the spot under my eye, and it was sent to the lab. After about an hour or so, he returned to say that all the cancer was gone, so they were ready to close the wound on my cheek. I was administered more numbing agent, and the doctor began to close the incision under my eye. It took nine very small and close-together stitches.

The intent was to avoid a scar on my lovely face. After he was finished, they were about to begin the same process for the mole on my back. Because of all my heart issues, I'm on a couple of blood thinners. The result is easy bleeding for even the smallest of wound. A simple cut from shaving, for example, may bleed for many minutes. As they were examining my back, the incision under my eye began to bleed fairly profusely. After several gauze pads were applied to no avail, it was decided to remove the stitches and cauterize the wound before re-stitching.

More numbing agent was again administered. Cauterizing involves burning the tissue to seal off the blood vessels. It was relatively painless, but the odor was enough to make me gag-- especially realizing it's one's own tissue one smells burning. After the cauterizing process, the wound was again stitched. It was successful. No excess bleeding.

After much discussion, the doctors and I decided not to do the Mohs surgery on the mole on my back. Rather, it will be examined at a future date to see what, if anything, is developing. The biopsy had not determined that skin cancer was present, but the mole just looked "funny" to the doctors. My head and eye areas were bandaged, making me look like a pirate, and we were on our way.

Of course, after the surgery, my eye looked like I'd been taken behind the woodshed. Nice and blackish purple, swollen nearly shut—it was a doozy. Relatively painless, but it sure looked horrible. I had to schedule an appointment at the Rockford VA outpatient clinic to have the stitches removed a week after my surgery. The stitches were removed easily, and the area has healed completely, leaving no discernible scar. So, I'm still looking good—certainly not average.

CHAPTER

FORTY

In mid-December, I received a call from the principal at Newman Central Catholic High School inquiring if I would be interested in a very part-time teaching position: one class, senior English, which is British literature. Newman is on what is called the block system. Students have only four classes each day, and a specific class meets every other day. For example, English is Monday, Wednesday, Friday this week, and Tuesday, Thursday next week. The classes are twice as long as a normal high school class, so at the end of a two-week cycle, a student has the same minutes of class time as under a system where class meets every day. It's especially great for classes involving set-up time such as science, art, music, and physical education. I was involved with the block system for years when I taught at Byron High School. Since I was classified as "standard" 100% disability, not "unemployable." I was eligible to accept this job. If I decided to take the position, I would be teaching one class from 8:00 to 9:22 every other day. That meant there would always be a three-day weekend. I agreed to take the position, starting with the second semester in early January.

My plans were slightly impacted once again by health issues, but this time it wasn't heart related. On the day after Christmas, I awoke to discover that both my eyes were swollen, red, and oozing fluid which was solidifying and quite literally "cementing" my eyes closed. I was compelled to use my fingers to peel open my eyes. I couldn't open them on my own. I went to the immediate care clinic and was told it was severe pink eye and was given some eye drops to use four times a day. After three days there was no improvement, so I went to the local hospital's emergency room. After a two-hour wait I finally saw a doctor who spent about thirty seconds looking at me and prescribed some different eye drops and some antibiotic pills. Several days passed with still no improvement, so I contacted my usual eye doctor in Rockford. An appointment was made for the next day. Unlike the other encounters, this time I was given a thorough examination utilizing a number of tests. Again, antibiotic eye drops were prescribed to be taken four times daily. Finally, with these new eye drops, the redness and swelling slowly began to improve. I was scheduled to return several days later for a check-up on my progress. The doctor administered several tests again and changed the prescription. Once again, I was taking eye drops 3-4 times daily. I was to return again in a few days.

When I returned this time, my eyes were greatly improved. The swelling was nearly gone, and the redness was almost gone. However, the doctor recommended I undergo a procedure to remove the crust on my eyelashes which had accumulated as a result of the "oozing" from my eyes. The procedure involved numbing drops in my eyes and a small device which looked somewhat like an electric toothbrush. A solution was put on the rotating head of the "toothbrush," and my eyelashes, both lower and upper, were scrubbed to remove the crusty residue that had formed. It was not a pleasant experience—far from average. As before I was to return for a follow-up appointment the next week. When I did, the improvement was amazing. The swelling was all gone, and only a small amount of redness remained in my left eye. The doctor changed the prescription of the eye drops once again. I was to use them 3-4 times a day and come back in a week. When I returned a week later, my eyes were even more improved. The doctor told me to finish the bottle of eye drops and I should be good to go—back to normal.

Fortunately for me, my teaching schedule of every-other-day gave me the freedom to attend all the doctor appointments.

CHAPTER

FORTY-ONE

It seems my battle is never-ending. On March 25, 2018, I was once again admitted to the hospital for AFib related issues. I had a scheduled appointment with my cardiologist. I was aware that I was retaining fluid. My weight had gradually been creeping upward to where I was again at 300 pounds. My legs had become so swollen it was painful to walk since my skin was so tightly stretched. I was listless, short of breath, easily tired. I felt yucky. In fact, I felt below average.

I was admitted to the hospital, hooked up again to an IV drip of Lasix, and began to pee. It was the same procedure as I'd gone through three times previously. I guess the good news is this time it had been seven months since this had happened. The other three times were only three months apart.

As before, after three days I was released having lost nearly 20 pounds. I felt much better as one can imagine. In the follow-up appointment a week later, it was determined that I'd have another cardioversion in June to attempt to get my heart beat back into rhythm. I'm looking forward to that possibility.

Another change the doctor decided to make to my meds is one called metozalone. It's a "steroid" for the Lasix which makes it even more powerful than normal. One of the nurses said, "It can get water out of a rock." I'm to take it thirty minutes before a normal dose of Lasix…and then get ready. I record the times I go to the bathroom after taking my metozalone, and it's typically 12-15 times in the next twelve hours. That's a lot of peeing. It's effective because I have lost as much as 2-6 pounds in a day of water weight.

CHAPTER
FORTY-
TWO

As previously mentioned, in October of 2016 I had had a cardioversion. It was a temporarily success for about ten days. Since that time, I've been living with the symptoms of AFib: shortness of breath, no energy, retention of fluid. It's been miserable. On July 2 of 2018 I had a second cardioversion. Once again it was declared a success. I'm happy to report that as I write this, over three months later, I'm still in normal rhythm. My shortness of breath is improved, and I do have more energy. I realize all that could change at any time, but so far, I'm happy with the results.

I'm back at the cardiac rehab facility three days a week. Treadmill, NuStep, arm crank—they're all part of the routine. I can tell the difference because my recovery time between exercises is much improved over pre-cardioversion days. My ability to walk is a little better, although I still won't win any races…unless it's against a toddler.

CHAPTER
FORTY-THREE

Since I've been through all these medical situations, some of them literally life-threatening, I've been asked numerous times how I maintain such a positive attitude. My friends, my family, my colleagues, even my nurses have asked. The truth is, I don't really know with certainty, but I think it's because I refuse to be average. I have chronic congestive heart failure with six stents, quadruple bypass surgery, and three heart attacks. I'm insulin dependent diabetic—five shots daily. I suffer from lupus. I'm at stage three kidney failure, and I've had skin cancer. No way in hell that's average.

My parents, I'm sure, were a factor. My dad constantly harped about always doing your best, and never giving up. In his inimitable way he used to say, "Even if you're picking shit with the chickens, be the best picker of the bunch." My Uncle Tuck, with his "backwoods" and old-school work ethic, was a great influence in my life. All my coaches in high school, college, and afterwards continually preached the concept of never quitting, never giving up. I guess positivity and persistence have become a part of my personality. All my military training and experiences—especially in

Vietnam—have reinforced the belief that fighting to the last breath and never giving up is simply what one does. My success in the business world is also based on hard work, organization, and refusing to quit. My college friend and teammate who espoused the "I'm not average" theory most certainly played a factor in my way of looking at life. I expect to do well in whatever I attempt. I'm willing to put in the time and work to achieve success—and I simply won't take no for an answer. That includes doing the work involved in rehabbing after a medical issue. My expectations are to be successful, to "win" at everything I attempt. No matter what the situation, I feel as if "I've got this. I can handle it." An average person may not, but I can. That includes battling lupus, heart attacks and stents, open heart surgery and complications, kidney disease, diabetes, skin cancer, eye infections, and anything else life throws at me.

I'm now married to a beautiful and caring woman named Fran. We are kindred spirits in so many ways. She was an incredible basketball player herself--she's in the Illinois Basketball Coaches Association Hall of Fame for her achievements. She's 6'1" tall and was a three-year starter for Sterling High School. During those three years, their won-loss record was 62-3. Personally, her career statistics were nearly a triple double. She averaged 14 points, 11 rebounds, and 8 blocked shots per game. They were the first ever Illinois Girls High School State Champions with an undefeated season during her junior year. Fran was a two-time All-State player. After high school, she accepted a full-ride scholarship to attend Illinois State University where she was a varsity letter-winner.

Fran now works as a day-care licensing representative for the Department of Children, Family Services (DCFS). She serves a wide geographic area and has nearly 100 day-care centers and homes she regularly checks on. She loves her job and is very, very good at it.

Because of her athletic background, and because she also coached high school basketball, there's no "wifely complaining" about watching sports on TV. She's an avid Chicago Cubs, Bears, Bulls, and Blackhawks fan. Her strength and help during my medical issues have been truly above average. Her love, understanding, and support have helped me to be above average.

I think in many ways, the success of my three children has helped me to feel above average. Their own accomplishments give me a great sense of pride. The fact that each of them has succeeded well above average in their own professions helps give me a deep sense of personal achievement as a father.

My oldest son, Jeff, graduated from the University of Notre Dame with a degree in business administration and a concentration in marketing. Since graduation, he has worked in the health club industry. He's currently Vice-President of Operations for Fitness Formula Clubs, where he oversees the day-to-day operation of an 11-club fitness chain with over 1,000 employees in the Chicago area. His wife, Noelle, worked ten years as a paralegal and event planner for a large Chicago law firm. She has a degree in Education from Northeastern University but is now a stay-at-home mom with their three children, Vaughn, Emma, and Jack.

My daughter, Kelly, has a degree in early childhood education from Loras College. She also has a post-graduate masters equivalency Waldorf Teaching Certificate. She's currently working on an Administrative Leadership Certificate. Kelly has worked in early childhood for twenty years including two long-term nanny positions in California and two years teaching Head Start in Alaska. She's worked with Waldorf Education for thirteen years, including five years where she ran her own Waldorf preschool. She is presently a middle-school teacher and administrator at the Waldorf School of St. Louis. Kelly is married to Michael Feary, who is an avionics engineer at Gulfstream Aerospace Inc., in the St. Louis area. She has one son, Rowan, who is now fifteen and a high school sophomore. They live in a suburb of St. Louis.

My youngest son, Jason, also lives in the St. Louis area. He graduated from Truman State University in Kirksville, Missouri, where he was an all-conference football player. Jason is a financial advisor and shareholder with Renaissance Financial in St. Louis. He does investment management and financial planning. His wife, Gina, whom he met in college, is an independent sales rep for Staples Promotional Products. She sells branded merchandise to Fortune 100 companies. They have three children: Samantha, Jackson, and Andrew.

I have succeeded at being above-average nearly all my life. I view being "average" as a curse. If you woke up this morning, you're average. Now, what are you going to do to be above-average? What can you say to be above-average? What can you think to be above-average? How can you be above average in your job? In your relationships with others? In my mind, how or why can a person be satisfied being average? I refuse to accept being average. I'm sometimes tempted to say, "If I can do it, you can, too." But that's simply not true. Not everyone is willing or able to put in the mental and/or physical effort to be above-average. It seems to me that the key to being successful in anything we do is to demand of ourselves that mere average is unacceptable.

SOMETIMES

I sometimes see things that others never notice.
It makes me think that maybe I didn't
See them after all.
Or that others don't know where to look.
But then, they never worry.

I sit alone and cry sometimes, because I feel I must.
If a man lives and dies, and no one ever cares or cries,
Why should he live?
But I wonder,
Does it count if he cries for himself?

Sometimes at night, when I'm the only one in the world-
When the sky is the ceiling and the grass is the carpet
And the world is all around me, close-
I know I won't die young.
Because I'm meant for more than this.
Even if it is all I have now.

Things are funny.
People Love,
Hate,
Die.
But I just sit-alone usually-and dream.

Charley P. Riney (written in 1967)

EPILOGUE

When my friend and teammate explained how he expected to live longer than the six months his doctors gave him because he was above average, I took that to heart. It's been a stabilizing and motivating philosophy for me for more than thirty years. I'm not average. I refuse to be average. I now have the opportunity to put the philosophy to the ultimate test.

In late July of 2018 I was once again hospitalized for fluid retention due to my congestive heart failure. My feet, ankles, and legs were again swollen to the point where walking was painful because the skin was stretched so tight. More seriously, my stomach had become distended from the fluid and eventually fluid had gotten into my chest making it difficult to breathe.

As before, I was given an IV of diuretics, but in two days I had only lost a few pounds rather than the usual fifteen or so. The doctors decided to try a different, stronger, diuretic which improved the rate of weight loss, but it was much slower than my previous experiences. I ended up spending a week in the hospital. The problem was compounded by the fact that my kidney function is declining at an alarming rate. When I lose the weight rapidly, the kidney function deteriorates.

Unfortunately, just three months later in mid-October, the same thing occurred. This time I was hospitalized for three days. Using the more powerful diuretic, I lost fifteen pounds in those three days. In the next three days at home I lost another five pounds. I'm told my kidney function continues to deteriorate, and I have an appointment with my nephrologist (kidney doctor) in November to begin the process of dialysis.

Back on May 3, 2018, I had a first-time appointment with my

cardiologist at the VA hospital in Iowa City. He's a brilliant young man, very impressive credentials—undergrad at an Ivy League school, med school at Vanderbilt University—and a direct to the point bedside manner—which I appreciate. After reviewing my civilian medical records from the previous years and interviewing me for over an hour and verifying that I had indeed been hospitalized four times (now six) in the past two years for heart related issues, he gave me some startling news. He informed me that a person with that history would normally be dead within a year! His goal, he said, was to help me beat that statistic.

In my mind I interpreted that to mean that an average person would likely live less than a year. But I'm not average. So, I'm now trying to follow his advice, dietary restrictions, exercise recommendations and everything else he diagnosed. I am determined that when May 4, 2019, comes around, I'll still be here kickin' it, because I'm not average. I refuse to accept that diagnosis because it's for the normal, average person.

If interested in having Mr. Riney speak to your club, team, group, or organization please contact him to schedule a presentation.

charleyriney@yahoo.com

MY MOM AND DAD ON THEIR WEDDING DAY, MAY 15, 1944.

MY DAD, ARTILLERY SERGEANT PAT RINEY DURING WWII.

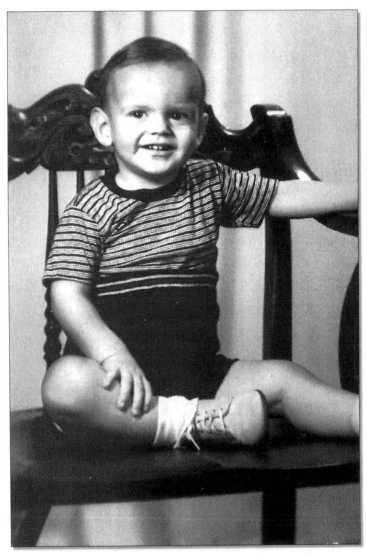

THIS WAS ME AS A VERY TALL TWO-YEAR OLD.

FIRST GAME MY JUNIOR YEAR. I SCORED 20
POINTS AND GRABBED 12 REBOUNDS.

ONE OF MY REBOUNDS DURING THE 1963 SEASON. I
LED TEAM BOTH JUNIOR AND SENIOR YEARS.

GRADUATES

Charley Riney
Class Vice-President

1963

GRADUATION PHOTO. I WAS LUCKY TO BE PRESIDENT
OR VICE-PRESIDENT ALL FOUR YEARS.

1966-67 LORAS COLLEGE BASKETBALL TEAM. TOM DEROUIN IS ABSENT. HE'S IN LORAS HALL OF FAME FOR HIS TENNIS EXPLOITS. THREE PHD'S AND A JURIS DOCTORATE SHOWN HERE.

GRABBING A REBOUND MY SENIOR YEAR OF COLLEGE.
COURTESY OF THE TELEGRAPH HERALD.

COACH BOB ZAHREN AND ME AFTER WE PULLED OFF AN
UPSET ON MY TWO FREE THROWS IN THE LAST SECONDS.

I WASN'T A STAR, BUT I HAD SOME GOOD MOMENTS.
COURTESY OF THE TELEGRAPH HERALD.

SENIOR YEAR CLEARING 6-2 FOR 1ST PLACE IN THE HIGH JUMP.

RED'S WORLD, THE 1972 IOWA STATE CHAMPION AAU TEAM. #25 IS GLEN VIDNOVIC, IOWA UNIVERSITY GREAT. ANOTHER IOWA GREAT FROM THE UNDEFEATED IOWA BIG TEN CHAMPION IS #23 CHAD CALABRIA.

THIS IS ME OUTSIDE DIAN (ZEE AN), HEADQUARTERS
OF THE 1ST INFANTRY DIVISION, IN LATE 1969.

JOE HEIPLE, MY ROOMMATE FRESHMAN YEAR AT LORAS.
SIX YEARS LATER WE SERVED TOGETHER IN VIETNAM
FOR TEN MONTHS WHEN THIS PHOTO WAS TAKEN.

ON THE BEACH AT VUNG TAU, VIETNAM, DURING IN-COUNTRY R&R.

VIETNAM IS A LONG WAY FROM IOWA.

1970 ON THE PERIMETER OF LONG BINH POST FOR MY TURN AT GUARD.

ONE OF MY BEST FRIENDS IN VIETNAM. JIM WAS DRAFTED
BY THE GREEN BAY PACKERS IN 1967 BUT THEN DRAFTED
BY THE ARMY AND NEVER PLAYED IN THE NFL.

JUST ANOTHER DAY IN VIETNAM.

KIDS IN AN UNNAMED VILLAGE. THEY ALWAYS ASKED, "GI, YOU HAVE CANDY?" THEY LOVED HERSEY CHOCOLATE BARS.

A GENERAL (WHOSE NAME I DON'T RECALL)
AWARDING MY BRONZE STAR.

MY BRONZE STAR CERTIFICATE.

ILLEGAL (NO CAMERAS ALLOWED) PHOTO TAKEN IN THE LOCC.

THE TWO UNITS I SERVED WITH IN VIETNAM: HQ,
1ST LOGISTICAL COMMAND AND HQ, USARV.

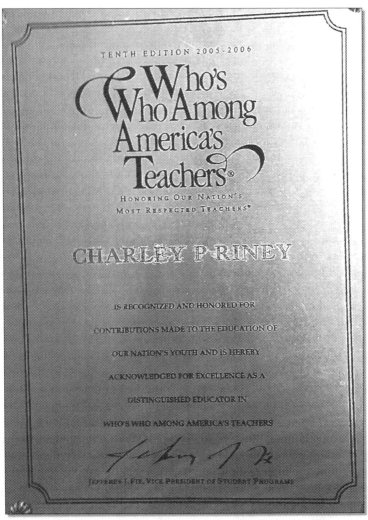

ONE OF MY FIVE *"WHO'S WHO AMONG AMERICA'S TEACHERS"* AWARDS. I AM VERY PROUD OF THESE.

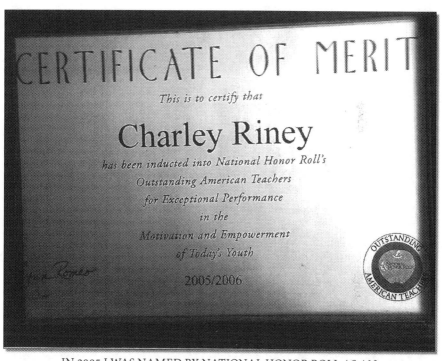

IN 2005 I WAS NAMED BY NATIONAL HONOR ROLL AS AN
EXCEPTIONAL TEACHER BECAUSE OF MY MOTIVATION
AND EMPOWERMENT OF STUDENTS.

IN 2004 I WAS HONORED TO BE INDUCTED INTO THE NEWMAN
CENTRAL CATHOLIC HIGH SCHOOL HALL OF FAME.

Most Inspirational Teacher

In recognition of excellence in preparing the next generation for academic achievement and leadership, this certificate of appreciation is presented to

Mr. Charles Riney

by

Western Illinois University

President

September 17, 2004

Date

TWICE I WAS HONORED TO BE SELECTED BY WESTERN ILLINOIS
UNIVERSITY AS A "MOST INSPIRATIONAL TEACHER."

DISTRICT (33 HIGH SCHOOLS) COACH OF THE
YEAR FOR THE 1979-80 SEASON.

Century 21

Country North, Inc.

Charley Riney
In-House Sales Leader

2008

2008 WAS A VERY GOOD YEAR FOR ME. I SOLD MORE OF OUR
OWN LISTINGS AT CENTURY21 THAN ANY OF THE OTHER
120+ AGENTS. NOT BAD FOR A PART-TIME AGENT.

MAY 23, 2009, FRAN AND I WERE MARRIED.
ONE OF THE BEST DAYS OF MY LIFE.

FRAN AND I AT CENTURY 21 AWARDS DINNER.

FRAN AND I AT A FRIEND'S DAUGHTER'S BLACK-TIE WEDDING.

TAKEN AT FRAN'S DAUGHTER SIERRA'S WEDDING IN 2016.

IN 2014 THE ROCKFORD AIRFEST SELECTED ME AS
ONE OF THEIR "HEROES" TO BE HONORED.

IN 2000 AT THE AGE OF 55 I COULD STILL SQUAT 450
POUNDS. NOT TOO BAD FOR AN OLD GUY.

AT AGE 54 I STILL HAD A SWEET JUMP SHOT. NUMBER 2 IS DENNY
HOFFMEISTER WHO PLAYED AT EASTERN ILLINOIS UNIVERSITY. WE
PLAYED THE GUS MACKER 3 ON 3 TOURNAMENTS FOR YEARS.

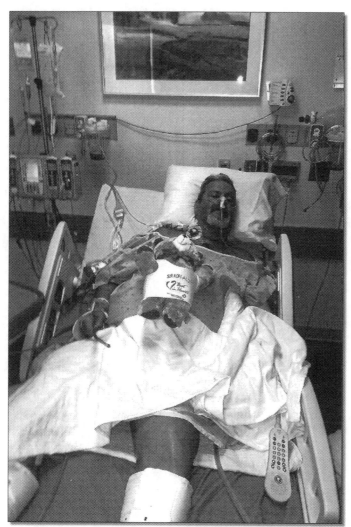

AFTER MY QUADRUPLE BYPASS SURGERY. DIDN'T KNOW
I'D BE OPENED UP AGAIN WITHIN 24 HOURS.

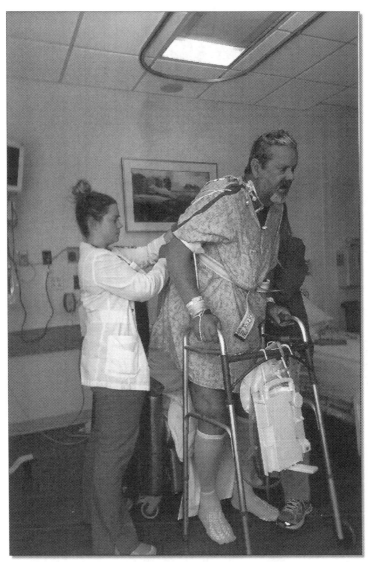

THIS WAS MY FIRST TIME ATTEMPTING TO STAND AND WALK
AFTER TWO OPEN HEART SURGERIES. IT WAS NOT A FUN TIME.

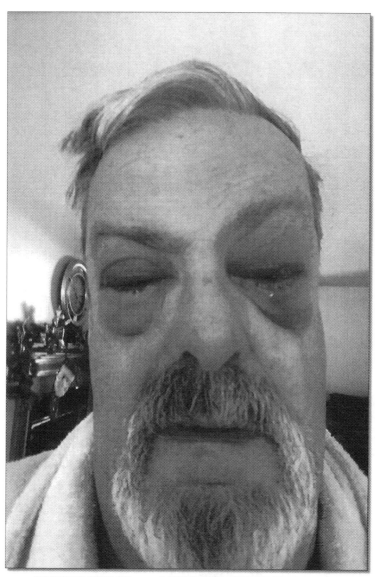

IN DECEMBER OF 2017 I SUFFERED AN EYE INFECTION.
IT ACTUALLY FELT WORSE THAN IT LOOKS.

I PAINT IN OILS AND ACRYLICS. NEVER BEEN
ABLE TO MASTER WATER COLORS.

I USUALLY PAINT LANDSCAPES, BUT I HAVE DONE A FEW OTHER SUBJECTS.

MAIN ENTRANCE TO THE KEOKUK NATIONAL CEMETERY.

TOMBSTONES IN THE KEOKUK NATIONAL
CEMETERY. SOME DAY ONE WILL BE MINE.

MY CHILDREN AND ME. JASON, KELLY, AND JEFF. FROM LEFT TO RIGHT

ABOUT THE AUTHOR

Charley P. Riney, a retired teacher and coach, has a degree in English from Loras College in Dubuque, Iowa. His graduate work in guidance counseling was done at the University of Iowa. He has previously published original poetry and several articles in athletic publications on coaching basketball and track. He and his wife, Fran, have six children and live in Sterling, Illinois.

Printed in the United States
By Bookmasters